THE SPARROW
SELECTED POEMS

Also by A. F. Moritz

Poetry
Here
Black Orchid
Between the Root and
    the Flower
The Visitation
The Tradition
Song of Fear
The Ruined Cottage
Ciudad interior
Phantoms in the Ark
Mahoning
Houseboat on the Styx
Rest on the Flight into Egypt
The End of the Age
Conflicting Desire
Early Poems
Night Street Repairs
The Sentinel
The New Measures
Sequence

As Editor
The Best Canadian Poetry in
    English, 2009
The 2010 Griffin Poetry Prize
    Anthology

Translation
Children of the Quadrilateral:
    Selected Poetry of
    Benjamin Péret
Testament for Man: Selected
    Poems of Gilberto Meza

Translation of Works by
Ludwig Zeller
Ludwig Zeller in the Country
    of the Antipodes: Poems
    1964–1979
The Marble Head and
    Other Poems
The Ghost's Tattoos
Body of Insomnia and
    Other Poems
Rio Loa: Station of Dreams
Woman in Dream
The Rules of the Game:
    Selected Shorter Poems
    1952–2008
For a Savage Love:
    Three Books

THE SPARROW

SELECTED POEMS

A. F. Moritz

Edited by Michael Redhill

ANANSI

Published in Canada in 2018 and the USA in 2018 by House of Anansi Press Inc.
www.houseofanansi.com

House of Anansi Press is committed to protecting our natural environment.
As part of our efforts, the interior of this book is printed on paper made from
second-growth forests and is acid-free.

22 21 20 19 18   1 2 3 4 5

Library and Archives Canada Cataloguing in Publication

Moritz, A. F.
[Poems. Selections]
The sparrow : selected poems of A.F. Moritz / A.F. Moritz.

Issued in print and electronic formats.
ISBN 978-1-4870-0302-9 (softcover).—ISBN 978-1-4870-0363-0
(hardcover).—ISBN 978-1-4870-0303-6 (PDF)

I. Title. II. Title: Selected poems of A.F. Moritz.

PS8576.O724A6 2018   C811'.54   C2017-904735-3
                            C2017-904736-1

Library of Congress Control Number: 2017947368

Cover and text design: Alysia Shewchuk
Typesetting: Sara Loos

Canada Council   Conseil des Arts   ONTARIO ARTS COUNCIL
for the Arts   du Canada   CONSEIL DES ARTS DE L'ONTARIO
                                            an Ontario government agency
                                            un organisme du gouvernement de l'Ontario

*We acknowledge for their financial support of our publishing program
the Canada Council for the Arts, the Ontario Arts Council, and the Government of
Canada through the Canada Book Fund.*

Printed and bound in Canada

For T.

CONTENTS

PART III: 1998–2000

from A Houseboat on the Styx (1998)

from Rest on the Flight into Egypt (1999)

PART IV: 2004–2008

PART V: 2012–2015

from Sequence (2015)

Coda

from Black Orchid (1981)

We Decided This Was All

Then we decided this was all: a birch forest on a border,
perhaps of Poland and Germany. And not in summer but
        when the sun
at noon is low in the south, and golden scraps seem caught
in a haze of twigs: shreds of a thin being that fled by night.

A man and woman, still on the verge of childhood, go
        walking there
and come upon a wire fence and the insolent grey
soldier with his gun. They turn back, the thought dies in them
to use the soft yellow leaves and needles for a bed.

Tomorrow their holiday ends and the train takes them back
to some quarter of sagging tenements ringed in with mills,
to work at a shop counter. The new ideas in their cafés
are already forgotten in Paris: freedom from God, the age of man.

As the century deepened, unbound from old delusions,
and the Bessemer converter, the pickling mill, gave way to
        the microchip,
we saw those lovers were Jews, were dead. And yet their lives
        had been
safe next to ours: malevolence was not so free in their day.

Elsewhere — in France, in America — men tried to excuse
        themselves
for being rich and happy. All is madness, they said. We suffer too.
Love takes many forms, all equal: enjoy the brief gift
when time grants you absence of pain.

When I came to myself under maple trees, King Arthur's book
        in my hand,
like a child I didn't yet know what we had decided. But was
that ignorance like a child's? Some children knew in the streets,
in knives, bloated bellies, brains ruined by hunger.

I wanted only the beauty of what is impossible,
unbroken love between men and women, earthly peace
in a country of marvels lost in flowering woods and fields.
But only the coming dissolution seemed inevitable and real.

This, and a desire to contradict everything
in a world so small. The words that I would say
would say how vast the world is when it is not mistaken
for everything, but is held in something else,

how safe it is when our love is not desperate
need for the only thing we have. But what were words to me
except a desperate, sole, luxurious love:
I was getting ready for nothing, present pleasure was enough.

So, now, many fragments of the word that was meant to save
lie in this room unknown to any. I am at an age when words
should be finished, and God only knows if such a word
exists and, though not speaking it, I at least will hear.

Sometimes I think of starting again, of slowly building
a small monument out of the things of my own life.
But in fact there are none, and no human desire can secure a work,
however modest: say, a circle of six pebbles on the ground.

PART I

1974–1983

Thinking About Dreaming

Suddenly the hammock wraps me up,
a new cocoon. The daiquiri approaches
twirling her spear
to enlist me in her troop of cars.

"Chrysalid of vengeance," says someone else.
Indeed, I am as enchanted
as the elements in a ticking bomb.

Every day my father shines his lamp
over the links of the chain,
a warder fingering bones on the floor.
It is all so clear, how the old ones are estranged.
I follow him. He puts on his white smock
and opens me up. Who knows what I was
before he showed me how a rope
strings a bunch of cans together?

The men are marching furiously, flies
upside down on the ceiling of the womb.
The patient women sleep like the flowering
of a shell thrusting a hole into a wall.

The old schoolteacher with her penis in hand
points out the light. Really, no one can wait
for the dark to come round again.

The moon will be bathing down in the wet woods.
I think I'll leave my hounds at home.
I think I'll go out to her and kiss her
and enter her as a fish thrown back.

Like Water

Already when the furred solidity of peaches
first meant to you a physical desire
that had no outlet, the former things
had come upon your heart. Only you
felt the age in the blank translucence
of those billion pebbles rubbed and whispered to
constantly by a weak surge.

And though I wanted to make plans for you
and spoke in your ear, the words were like the water
that you knew not as an emblem
of eternity but as the thing itself:
tired, desperately unable to die,
softening space to a silver mirror,
already as old as you will have to be.

In Winter

The swirling tire ruts in the frozen mud
of the field outside our window: these
seemed to us emblems of the road
we thought we had been looking for and found
smashed like a rusted spring. The spring

is coming, will turn to a dawn-coloured
broth these brittle sculptures
the motorcycles left us as a sign
for our conversion. You look across
to the trees. If you are caught, it isn't

within walls, behind windows, in the flesh.
It's in the seeing that already finds
beyond this another winter, where
the changes, though noticeable, are not
of the least importance to anyone.

Here

We are as young in sunlight as the stones
that will live almost forever, we are as old
in shadow as the stones that have had to wait
almost since the beginning. Amber lights
open from time to time in a mask of cloud.
Between are brown moments in the coal-dust air.
To cease is not permitted here.
To complete something is not permitted.
Out of the river climb elongated musics,
oddly shaped shrieks of light,
walls of brittle, unmortared bricks.
Staring littered and sunken in the hard
mud of the banks, the third eyes are glass.

The Art of Poetry

The alarming radio of morning spoke
of eastern wars. But the same voice, changed,
came also from a blue tulip by the bed
with news of a wanderer underground.
So dreams died. How could we sleep again,
be scissors closing to cut
the flower of intellect from the images?
A new light was changing the kinds of space.
Walls that had hovered in darkness set themselves
and whitened like clay baking. The chandelier
appeared in the watery round mirror,
its featureless three bulbs glowing within
the halo of gold foil. The curtains moved,
cascade of roses under a light warm wind,
and in the spreading clearness
all was deformed from what it clearly is —
the faint clashing
of curtain hooks was the music of deformity.
Just as a man who stoops down in the street
may be made, struck by the sun, a headless knot
where all that tends to death convenes,
then he stands up again
in glory, human and common —
so dawn read for a moment
the lost allegory of our room.

The Uses of the Past

In the beginning is a light cloud floating
through an open door that stands there
in the middle of nowhere. The hill accepts the vapour.
And all at once everywhere something was
forging without perceptible aim
through the golden meadow
to the various ends of earth.
So the evolution of desire
extends its precious pile of mute bearings
to the circular motive
of unanchored colonies of weeds living on air.
In a sense we had been turned to nothing, in a sense
snatched from the path of those hard lights
that come rushing out of mist and disappear,
leaving only a smashed body on the sidewalk.
Now there is a motion in the air, a fear,
a sense of something missed and missed again.

And so with all its baggage, its maimed gestures,
on the balcony in the dim distance
the soul tenderly emerges
from the rumour it has been so many years.
Of humble origins, it turns to do something
for the residue camped below in the muddy field.
A phosphorescence from this moment draws itself up.
The black surface swallows a shining bolus
meteorically altering unruffled night.
Now what can anyone see up there but a dwarf
bursting from the empty ghost of his form?

Shade

Before you were born, beauty's summer died.
Now at times it brushes you
with its abstract wing, like a virtue,
something from a world where bodies have no bodies,
are as real as names and produce no tears.

Here the sounds of the beautiful ideas,
heard or unheard, sit looking down through mist
at leaves that are browning or will brown,
and on both sides of the window the water
slowly condenses and rolls earthward.

So a thought of time dwelling in a timeless place
will fall, if a tree dares to dash across the sun.
A blow of shadow strikes your sleep in whitened light.
But has your day come too soon, stayed too long,
that the skin is dry now, an expectation of flame?

Again the image: days passing beneath oaks
to nothing but further days, further knowledge
of the sky held in fingered leaves:
it empties you into confusion.
Metamorphosis is pain and in pain
you look now through the eyes of some animal.
Of all that is visible, nothing remains
marked out as yours in the soft, darkened afternoon.
Far away the tree-aisles dim
to nights that, entered, are not nights
but other limbs of this day
held in stroking shadow.

And that ancient being, you, sole citizen
of the shadow, waits, echoing with muted light;

alone, cannot pronounce itself alone,

expecting someone, expecting pleasure:

nor shall you brag it wanders in death's shade.

Morning Fragments

The ledger vanishes in the flood again.
The blue bowl pours, warm liquid fills this air,
melting the block of ice that held you.
Now vast blindness is a legend that eddies away
into crumbling warehouses,
the hearts of evergreens,
your throat.

What survives there is the wish to recall
the clear plan of your days
and of all to come. And the morning fragments,
growing visible, seem to rebuild themselves
out of twilight, mildew, and melancholy
toward an edifice still darkened in you:
as if this new hour were not yet morning
but the ghost and messenger of morning.

And were you here yesterday already?
Did your feet, as now, mark out a track
through the glassy moisture of the lawn,
and even then were you following
faint prints of a day before? Today
you determine to remember everything.
You will know at last if the sun ages
or is created every dawn
out of nothing at the surface of the sea.
You will know if this dayspring is eternal
or lies on a heap of others,
a page just turned, reversing all.

And meanwhile night has sunk as a hedge
sinks into distance as you walk away.
Voices were making explanation behind it,
something you might have understood, some secret
of a former life. But glowing spaces outward,
poplar spires and domes of the willows,
were newly before you then, they drew you on,
so that now you will never know what was being said,
if something is lost forever,
or if much, happily,
is put behind you and forgotten.

Food for Three Days

Dumpling soup and sardines on crackers.
Sardines and salami on crackers.
The sun impassive in the wet tar.

Sardines and salami on crackers.
A little sugar in the canned beans.
The sunset impulsive in the streaked window.

A little sugar in the canned beans,
a dozen peaches in a polished window,
like the sunset of morning

a dozen peaches in a polished window.

Anniversary in the Private Room

Despite the mystical design of a lost religion
that seals the wall where a window ought to open,
it seems to us now that time goes past
more slowly outside, in expectation
of stopping in the garden for which we plan.
It seems that, by the river, a man says to his wife,
"The blueprint I gave you
was a tracing of your mother's skeleton.
In those days of our sad youth proclaiming
war between knowledge and desire,
we had never been anywhere but all over the world.
And we wrote those laws that night."

We nod our heads. They might have known
that part of us is night,
how it turns over in its grave and is recalled
by this accident to morning.
Everything gets one last chance,
just as tomorrow will. And though your foot
slips now and then with a faint cry in the tremor
of an earth built slowly of disappointed fathers,
still you press a seed hole and drop in
a motive for the words to come,
as immense as allegorical temples
in the landscape of the body.
And in earliest spring, already, the tiny ear-flowers
hear the verse of bees arrowing from future time
to wet their feet in this excited dust
and spread it everywhere, and smear it
all over the bleached pelvises of cities.

Meanwhile, nothing disturbs your joy, O queen
of this endlessly inventive melody,
human aria for which
the circular left hand of the orchestra
has long waited, perfecting itself
in the grievous beauty of its flaws.
Nothing, except that now and then your voice
breaks when you are suddenly laid asleep
by the sight of a dead man on a bone-white street
laughing with friends as he enters an office door:
for no one ever appears far off
on our horizon here, approaching our gate
through the telescopic clarity of this air.
How lonely you sometimes seem
in the infinity of your unknown hope
walled up in silent prayer. And the insolent,
unyielding hieroglyph closes the lips
around the promise of being as you are.

Ulysses en Route

Rock. Sun and rock.
And all day long naked feet
falling on the rock and the sun
falling like a drop of lead into the brain.

So I retain the image of the meagre world
that now amid crowded flotsam
in shipwreck, in absence, I desire:
not as relief but as
the true adventure, dusty
spring, spaces where the cypress
denies denial, hurling waves
upward of blue-green foamed to gold.

It is to be unborn
in branching tunnels,
this custody of the wind's treasure
that must not be touched, this knowledge
of swine born of the intercourse
between men and the sun's power, this wisdom
from the powerless dead. But am I lifted
back toward that first sun mark
on these upheavals of the torn bursting crest,
in the circular storm that rolls
in night's groundless sphere?

And still, I am an idea,
this is a breath of envy
to men who hear of these adventures
and have not looked in their own house.
Banal to me as glances in a mirror,

as strengths unacknowledged, are these courses
in the world's belly,
regions like bowels serving the lighted flesh,
these palaces
and courtesies hidden in the supporting
ocean, huge parodies of man,
equations of harmony and sleep.

I'd return to that blazing
where slime is turned to brick. O for sleep
to pour again
from walls catching fire at noon,
for summers stretching like a knotted rope,
for my arm bent to all the broken
stones that wasted me, strong illusion
of boredom, spur of this plunge
into the lungs of this blue breast's swelling.

And not at all can the jealousy
that is yours, who watch, left behind
on stretching beaches, redeem for me
the journey. Now I know
how to breathe the golden dust
of my threshing floor and not be turned to gold.
In the fields, thrown by the sun
more invincible each day, I could laugh
like a young wrestler now
foreknowing an end to his weakness.

Poem

The unheralded mystery of spring
forces its will again on the herald flower.
In the thicket I pause to remember.
February was my mentor in misery,
that hollow pamphlet from yellow skies,
basin of dead sparrows.
I am a glove on an absent hand
and speaking, writing are nothing but the dream.
Don't try to say they are anything more than dream.
Whether or not there is such a thing as time,
I am this window on night's senseless palette,
which is already the portrait
more perfect than the face.
Across the torn darkness
I am this anarchic scrawl,
this wake of a restless scalpel.

The Naturalist

When my heart first began to stutter
so no one could understand it
(they guessed it was prophesying death),
then I had second thoughts. I moved
here to this slope in a line of mountains
facing another line of mountains
like men facing women at a dance.
Eighty-eight years in the city. I recall
a phrase: "up and down" or was it "back and forth"?
And something about tires, revolving and revolution,
and the gratefulness of sleep, the fact that
everyone I knew was slipping away,
building up a mask of wood. So little
remains of that, like the sweat of breath on a window
shrinking to give the view again.
Now I plan to sit here and watch the weather
roll down this aisle to the valley,
as today. Everything is reversed
from what it was. Lighted paths of rain
wind as though upward from the overcast
into a ragged green sky: the trees.
Unmoored islands, the clouds
pass in a rhythm,
blue spaces between. A sun comes out
from their trailing edges: a kind of morning
climbing from horizons overhead
toward a zenith in the earth. Today
there were seven mornings in the storm.
I plan to sit here: maybe the chances
will give two years to compare with one another.
I've heard of "new growth," the intangible

difference of one spring from the last,
which evades memory, too small,
too simple for the mind.
I wonder what I will make of it?
One ring closer to all I want?

Black Orchid

A black orchid convokes bees
at your body's centre,
a stem of urine
connects it to the ground.
Near where you stand, the fishes
leap up an arc of light
and hang in a rainbow
over the disgorging cleft.

We are sad while we live here.
We hate this summer for the fleshy children
who force themselves as food into our eyes
closed toward the future.
Then the summer swells,
it will not last forever.
How we long for deliverance
as the lizards show and disappear
between the white rock
and the leaves: the lizards, blue and green,
little replicas of how the sky's
acid meets and etches
the temple of the palm forest.

And looking into the region
of that burning, with what desire
earth is moved
continually to pour itself.
The fountain raises its head
and with water's passionate vengeance
loses all
to colour the dry rock with these flowers.

The Pauses

As children we would search
the ground for signs,
certain a language had been planted there
by purpose, its recovery to lead
to a destination, some knowledge
deposited for us in a hidden place.
We read broken twigs in the woods,
spots of paint on the grass,
or blood. Openings among the stems
of dense bushes along the creek
to us were a trail, now useless,
where someone had passed long ago.
We followed arrows,
numbers, crude signs
painted on sidewalks
across the city: they turned
and re-entered themselves, circles
that later we were told
were marks of men planning sewers.
And we came to unexpected things:
a tunnel of woven brush
floored with soft mulch that led
to a round hall of higher bushes
filled with green light; a shelf
of the creek bank thrust out under
a veil of vines from the trees,
where we saw the bass
pierce a reflection of the sun
among reeds. There the huge willow
was a faceless virgin weeping
over the stream while we stood

in the pit of her eyes and lips.
Or if one of us went out alone
in the earliest light, often
he would find a place of total still,
though not silence: the fly
and goldfinch spoke from far off
to his isolation in tall grass
under a clear bell
of sunlight turning to light
all impressions of all bodies.
A strange idleness always met
the adventurer led by chance traces
(the only fruits of our careful science)
to ends of calm looking, hearing, feeling,
of warmth passing into the body
at the base of the neck, of long moments
melded to a scent of weeds
in the memory. And was this in fact
all we wanted the signs to point at? —
this peace as common as air,
yet entered only when a pause
that seemed endless
fell, strengthening the curious one
to abandon it again.

The Wasp

At noon
sleeping beside a pine tree
I was awakened by a huge cross
labouring through the air
roaring loudly
its head turned toward the ocean.
With what misery
what fortitude what drowsiness
a wasp on that last warm day of October
picked its way
in the castle of magnetic needles
bristling toward a million points
each indicating snow.
But at last it fell to the earth.
"When" it asked me
"will you quit waking up
scaring away the star of June
from your forehead
the clear vista
high paths among mountains of water?"
And indeed armies of ghosts
were fleeing
across the shaking grass
were tearing the woods apart
in their panic
spilling into the river.

Stabbing

We found you on the subway stair
struggling for breath, filled with twenty wounds,
blood fighting with the voice in your throat.
As the train had rattled forward
and left you there (progress
is the same as ever, but wrinkled now,
with falling teeth), it had happened
almost in silence in the passage upward
to night and the towers
that indicate and obscure the stars.
Twenty wounds: four times the number
of your senses, twice the number
of your body's natural openings. New doors
cut in you by a misery grown fierce
at what little it receives.

You were a symbol as he took you,
and now are a girl dying.
Like so many other mutilations
done for the symbol's sake: lips
and foreskins mangled, false channels
opened inward, limbs and bodies
cut away in our desire
to conform ourselves to the red coming out
of day from night. And afterward we climbed
all night long past trees and clouds
till morning, the snow and blinding glare.
We were going to see God and redeem him
from the sacrifice he is said to need from us:
our enemy's heart, or a purchased girl
flung in the well, taking our daughter's place.

In the thin air our lungs were bursting
and the cold made us cry. We wanted
to consume pain without conceiving more,
to discover through long labour
the formula of transmutation.

And all this time in the city behind us
is your ordeal. The murderer
desperate to release the secret in you,
to make you speak and kiss
more deeply than your body tells him
is possible, to force a way in
for all that knocks and is not opened to.
Or so I say, trying to understand.
More simply I say he hated you
and wanted you to die. He could not see
what you are. And at once I desire
revenge, to commit on him what he has done,
inheritor of the centuries of false instincts,
rites founded on a mote in the eye,
the stupid illusion of evil. So the circle
reasserts its power: longing
to tear the miserable human things apart,
to drag knowledge from their beauty
that won't stop destroying itself.

Despite all effort continually in me
victim and murderer perform
all that was done in those dull lights underground.
In me without end, without physical sign,
the gift is also anger and a blow,
acquiescence is greed, possession
of cherished flesh is a wall.
The days eat amputations, the human body

digests its pain. And you now and he
are fragments in my mouth.

Romance

There are houses I love looking at: grey stone,
which trees surround and which sweat water
in dreary weather like the rocks near a falls.
The upper stories seen from a block away
through gaps in the leaves are ruins, and on the roof
the air in winter presses with the same
weight and captured hues as ice. And if
you stand up there behind the balustrade,
the lidless slit of the bay must stare
into your eyes, and a dull gleaming that rhymes
faintly with the snow in the dim street
curls around your ankles. But the huge elm
that hangs above you at last forgets
its black scratching on a crumpled paper
and becomes a head again. You see up now
through intricacies, out past an avalanche
of green hair to blue pieces of some other place.
Though this house wraps gleams of polished glass
around itself, through the transparent cloth
still it reminds you of a face the way
a woman's body does: a face
with one expression, a round-mouthed gaze,
that seems about to utter a long formless sound.
But when a man with a Great Dane opens
the door and leaves, he is an idea
materializing in the form of fruit
on its tongue. It is this man, the owner,
who in September sits in the curved turretlike
third-story study above the lake.
A mass of strings from his radio is a current
that rushes him under the phosphorescent roof

of a low tunnel underground. The foghorns
and the clank of railroad cars fall through
his windows the way accidents create music.
It seems that huge chunks of rock tumble behind him
and change in falling to birds and flying reptiles
of hollow and tinted blown glass: they ring
like half-drunk glasses of water touched
by silver rods. He goes to sleep
and is cast up where the sun pulls roses
from the carpet. All day passing over,
it calls on different corners: the stags running
on the stairway wall, a fierce table
holding stones in its claws. At noon the old
lady sealed in flannel and the girl
in her jersey bathing suit sit like clothes
thrown over chairs in the garden. Narcissus
in the birdbath stoops, a centrepiece,
displaying how he hangs more fragilely
than a leaf, though made of stone. And soon
they're asleep, I forget how the house reminds me
of water streaming from a stone carving
in cold rain. I approach the wrought iron gate
for a better view of the garden. And now the owner
with his black dog comes back around a corner
and shouts, "What do you want here?" What I want
is like this never to be finished looking.
What I want is poetry like this house.

The Ground

1

Now your body
is the forest you wander through,
never encountering a limit.

There's no one here. You meet
an eye balancing on a nerve, looking up,
an ear that bows itself to the moss,
a bush of hands, unmoving lips
clinging to tree trunks.

Are there people nearby, concealed
behind the screen of air?

They own plots for temples here
but no one comes to build.
No conversation. Formless areas
to be entered: sleep and waking,
night and shade.

You roam the streets of a blueprint
inscribed in the white ground.
Only ferns rise,
suggesting it, hiding it.

2

The clay fragment of a wall
on which the plan was written
in a language you don't know:

"…in him
and he in you…"

Do you remember it,
was it something you found one day
and forgot, only to think of now?

Or did a dream construct it
from desire?

A ruin drops a seed. Or a stone
where no one but the accidental wind
has scratched a note
builds in you,
in the form of a ruin
overgrown with moss and vines,
the idea of a temple.

But the stars
and the spaces among stars
are only an ear
and you are the sense of hearing:

aroused by this hint, perfectly still,
you strain within yourself
for a city, a people,
a voice that is not raised.

3

Something goes through the world
continually raising and letting fall
the voice, the hammer, the glass of wine.

From far away, it is a man
dreaming underneath a tree.
Approaching, you enter
a city where all the walls
are doors open. Music
is synonymous with night.

As shade waters the light,
talk waters quietness.
Night and day succeed.

The maple tree sees the gleam
of a sleeper preparing for bed
in a house's eye. The wood
and stone tell each other
"good night" and both are seeds
of a dream that prepares itself
within the sleeper.

The corridor of morning air
opens on a work site
where the worker reaps diamonds
from his brow.

They purchase the opening
of flowers in a season of fruit.

4

A bone tinkers with a watch,
turning it back
before hands, before metals,
before number and time.

The bone smiles.
An old woman's smile
to the young is always half malign:
sunlight on western windows,
water falling.

But the bone will tell you
it wants to be a girl again
as always: perfectly young,
perfectly naked and unafraid.

A huge form
that does not live as living men
will come again and remind her,
"This is how men live."

A wind blows the ground
from under your feet
into a dark box. You bequeath
whatever will remain of you
to silence and night.

But a rumour of talk keeps playing
from the midst of the disaster.
And out of the faint hubbub
your own voice turns
from the other voices a moment
and asks you,
"What do you think you are?"

In the night, laughter and rags
of music from the house
step out into the spaces
under the wet trees.

5

Come out of the forest,
where you have buried yourself.
Here are the figures
that give you its leaves for hands.

Do not be angry with me
that I am married now.
In a dream I fell
back past the cage of lashes
and bodies split at the joints.
I fell into this bed
with what seemed a motion of ascent.

In the garden are ears to hear you,
eyes to see, lips to respond.
The strings of your ears and eyes
and brain will grow proportionate.

You stand in the breast of a dead man.
Bur I preceded and I follow you
and it is only the earth
covered with moss.
The social roots build there,
drawing from all directions
fruit and flower that decide
with sap of the unbidden emissaries.

The threat is made of fear.
Nothing is idle, nor even
a rock lying in an airless chest.

6

Voices
conversing nonchalantly
about what is...
Who's speaking? Where
is that celebration?

Absence is your trousseau,
the tuxedo of the spouse.

Bur the spouse has taken you,
you are together
where those voices are, while here
still you see silent things alone.

Your intercourse is only
two sentences, motionless,
naked side by side:

"We are together here."
"Where are you?"

Everything is completed
and you wait,
because you don't find the way,
no one comes to find you.

And someone else,
scarcely moving, says, "I am
in wood, in water...
Slip into my breast,
be lost in me."

But you don't hear him. Still
waiting for someone lost,
you say, "I am the ground —
inhabit me."

The Underground

*A poet who fought against occupying forces during World War II
responds to the criticism that, because his work stands for freedom in
his now totalitarian country, he is encouraging the enemy and thus
inviting nuclear war.*

Where is the world that lives? I've seen
the metal nipples measuring out
exact excretions of ground meat
into little cans...and the cattle
chained so that they can't move,
because they have been bred for so much flesh
and so little bone, to move
might break the pelvis, spoiling the meat:
so many, a whole race of fat
in an infinite corridor of stalls,
dropping dung on one conveyor,
eating continually from another.

I remember when the tanks passed through here,
crushing the hedges, ignoring the roads
already drawn through the orchards, the vineyards,
smashing the grapes — to make
a wine of misery — into the soil.
And in the gaps between the tanks, the men
with submachine guns and flame throwers
to fill out the solid advancing line
of death.

And yet they passed like ghosts:
through us, terrifying us, sending us
to bar ourselves in our houses,

carrying off many to the dead;
strengthless nonetheless, ineffectual,
a presence desperate to repossess
body and blood but consigned to shadows
and the conquest of shadows.
They made a shadow of the day
and tried to seize us there. But it was we
who disappeared, our world that vanished
during the day into calm villages
that made bread, composed prayers to Hitler,
saw their inhabitants taken.
Then at night we were in the hills
and existed once more, a dream world
that was abolished in the blinding shadow dawns
and rose again each dusk. And we
passed through the conqueror, as the living
pass through the dead.

No city was ours, no plain of farms,
no lines of tracks or wires
across the mountains. We held
no bridges over the rivers, no ships
or ports. The microscope and telescope
were theirs, the radio, the offices full of records,
the road and the trucks. And still
I wrote and my friends read, the words
scratched on cheap re-used papers
or repeated from camp to camp
in the caves where the fires were hidden.
How the absence of desks, of schools,
of many books, swelled our memories.
The words took the place of towns and fields.
So we would strike, and they
would cry, "Where is this world?"

finding another heap of their grey brothers
uniform, motionless, flecked with living blood
as if partially redeemed.
Solid bodies, men of flesh
we stood among them, untouchable.

This has happened. Yet they tell me
that words — which demand the people
should have what is theirs and was stolen,
should have it now—
must mute themselves lest these walls
be broken up and the fragile plant,
poetry, be the first to die.
If fire covers the whole earth
we will write, until the poison
invisible in the water
dissolves our bones. Our children
will write until the scales
bind their wrists, and the thumbs
drop from their hands grown claws.
We will read until the air eats our eyes
and then listen, remember, recite. Among us
the city will be built,
will spread from the speaker's lip
to the ear of the listener. Perhaps
no human hand will ever again
touch stone with power, but in the word
even the dead who invented death will rise.

A Narrow Silent Throat

How many nights eaten by rain
have I sat here, dreaming of the world,
this world which is, facing a blank wall,
the sound of ruining water?

Or dreaming by day when dust
filled the throat and the dry light
burnt all strength from the eyes:
a dream of night with its grateful moisture
out of the sides of the air,
its repose of trees and hedges, its gift
of music in running water?

Dreaming in suffocating nights
of a noon on wooded slopes:
breathable flame, agate that quenches thirst,
and the excellent shape of a maple leaf,
its shadow among a million shadows
conferring a just degree
of darkness upon day: the vegetable
humanizing the light.

Dreaming of a life still possible
in an anguished moment,
a narrow silent throat
where one by one, pulsing and shining,
the unbodied elements pass.

Loud Light and Quiet Light

Loud light and quiet light,
nights filled with chaos
and nights of emptiness... There was a power
emerging from behind our skulls
to make a blue insistent fire, as cool
and still as a frozen eye,
of some blank thing: maybe a tiny stone
wounding our feet. We lay inert
in that force which, working through, made
of the same dying bee, its drone
in a warm day crossed by frigid veins,
an inexhaustible chamber
and a meagre sign, a half-voiced word
falling
from decayed lips, imitating
by its obscure descent what it would say.
How is it that one day redeems the world
and the next throws it into hell, which a moment ago
could not exist in a universe too benign?
How without moving,
without having any hands,
did you and I lay hands on the world and move it,
so that the cricket gaily preached
unrepeatable truths that will never come again
from its perch on an old stove half submerged
in the stream? Or grasshoppers rose
into the light and like arrows
shot to tall flowers and fastened there
while something resembling a human body,
brown and soft, dropped
from a twisted apple tree into mud.

This world, aloof from us, where we two are
the most helpless, the most motionless
of all the particles, our eyes
pools of water where the flat sky comes
to curve, to rejoice,
turn to nothing, and cry.

Dark Man

I am the dark man, so dark
that in shadow or memory you would say
my flesh grows green.
When the light flickers under towering
oaks and willows, it seems to you that light
pierces me also, that there are blue
spaces in my chest and deep in me
a quivering, an unseen rushing, and a family
of chaotic notes shot with quick rhythms and melodies.
I too, like the lawn in the park,
have my tones of liquid ash and gold
that move across me. And sometimes at the end
of a lane of trees I seem to walk
into noon's darkly striped face as a suicide
fades into the bright sea.
Or if you stay close to me till evening,
you will lose me then, when you turn to look
at the mounded black and orange clouds
lying in the west at the field's edge
above the heads of the trees. You notice I am gone
but at once your question is lost in other questions:
what is the source of night, does dark gather
and mount from the hedges, from basements,
the woods, the interiors of spruce; or does it fall,
does shadow fall, this shadow as large as the earth...
and what is it to be deprived of light?

And when you are with me, you wonder at the source
of my wealth and my idleness. A sound
of running water at my feet reminds you
of gardens under harsh suns, Provence, Palestine

or Africa. You think of a wine farmer,
nobles of Sicily, an ancient house
where the last son oversees a green remnant
of former holdings. A man with nothing to do,
keeping to his shade and his streams
in a dusty country, where villages of dust cling
to mountains of dust and the people
sit staring at white walls: the street, the land, the sky.
A man who has learned all languages, knows
all literature and music, studies the stars
and writes without signing the work.
Yet for all this you confuse me in your thought
with an idea of the field, wild grass in motion
sprinkled with mustard flowers and apple trees.
And to watch me as I pass through open doors
onto the lawn, into sunlight, between
peonies as between torches,
is for you to see me naked
as though you surprised a boy in private woods:
only the tips of my ears are covered
by my dark hair that captures close to you
the light in twisting rivers.
And my feet too are invisible, sunk
in seasons of needles and leaves.

And in your thought we are still there together
much later when, the lights lit and the screens closed,
I sit at the piano. You would say you are alone with me,
despite the others, and the notes
of Liszt and of Alkan, warmth chased with cold,
fall and dust across us. First you hear them
above, striking the leaves like light fingers,
and then at last they reach down, refreshing us,
releasing the savours from plants and from the earth.

A Natural History of Words

I almost recall the origin of these words;
on a night like the interior of coal,
landscape of shadows, although no light existed
to make it possible, no objects to cast it forth.
There was a pond with a dark internal fire,
a half-moon in the polished sky.
And a rim of low hills with above them
identical dark clouds that swelled
from their own inverted ground. It was a mirror
gazing in a mirror, and the one faulty symmetry
a being pierced by unmeaning whispers,
flooded with echoes.
Crying reflections: they plundered
a rib from lonely contentment, the old days
of silence and the sun
thrust into the quiet eye
on the blade of a pine needle:
a child's silence, all comfort and wildness
where at noon seeds and withered hands
and pyramids fell without sound
in the shadow of offices.

Then the dead returned but not in their own forms,
fire and cold which kill men became a man.
Never again would I fail to speak
to the many-levelled city of bees,
or fear to trust my boat
to the ocean dissolved in evening.
Sometimes, between two woods shrinking in mist,
the whole earth seems to appear
in an almond of light,

suspending itself just above the ground,
from its fingers spreading the roads of the visible.

In all flesh, all mineral, all haze
and the most perfect clearness
there is speaking: conversations remembered.
But of the words, the speakers, what they said,
nothing remains, only a tone,
a shape to be filled with what occurs to us:
perhaps sadness, pride, desire,
love with resignation or triumph:
something that mingles with matter
and moves freely at the core.
The birds draw it out in their beaks,
it's the filament with which they link
the trees and the open spaces, afternoon and dusk;
it's the new path they invent
through this ancient park to which each second
restores a wilderness
greater than maze or mystery: a pleasure
planted here long ago
so there could be no end to understanding.

The Owl

Good luck that summer, dodging among the clouds,
followed me like some owl that for my sake
had forsaken the wet dark evenings. From his wings,
the feathers snowed down on everyone I knew.
Loving women, good money, and plentiful ease
touched my friends as I passed, and their talents
dipped a toe in the gold that runs
in the air's veins. My brother
was taken up by the spectre of my luck
and lifted across the Pacific to Japan
to bring the emperors knowledge of the piano
and of machines that lighten burdens and carry learning
beyond the sea. Everywhere in strange and happy mixture
I seemed to hear the notes of Beethoven
proceeding gaily and solemnly above the heads
of the feudal lords down the lanes of cryptomeria
to the Toshogu Shrine. The very clouds
where good luck hid itself were now
the exhalations of tea drunk to my brother.
I recognized them when they rolled over the mountains
to stir with their blazing sticks the stone
city of Guadalajara in its tall cup.
I saw the ancient alphabet in its sky,
and found a parchment there more full of water
than the plumpest reed, which bleeding as I wrote
began to wash false slogans from the walls.
What can I say of huge marriages beginning
in the smallest rooms, of flowers coaxed by my wife
from the deep shade,
happy sheep ripe for slaughter,
a dead voice crying from forty years ago,

freshening the western light with death?
I seemed to be on some liner on a calm ocean
far from any land, and this owl where no owl could be
lit on the bridge, right up where the sun is blinding.
Then I sat in a cemetery on the steps
of a large tomb, an imitation temple
with a padlock on its door against vandals,
the trees interpreting the late sun for me,
adding moist green and black, the owl
hidden somewhere among them. I thought how its feathers fell
and it seemed to me they were snow, that winter had come.
In the neighbourhood all the roofs were covered with snow,
the streets were filled, the drifts came up to the sills,
and the snow gleamed, crossed with bony shadows
in the moonlight and the soft yellow lamplight
from the bedroom windows, huge like descending stars.
Even there, at rest in my tree, was the white owl.

Only Deeper

The brass mountains fell apart
and bridges cried, deposed
in the empty grammar
among statues' painted eyes,
pieces lying
between plaster fingers,
in the crooks of knees. That
is our wisdom: nothing
must be, the organs
are seized with an idea or mood,
transcend the body and destroy it,
and every bone with its thin
layer of dust prepares
its widowhood:
for the loved ones who just left
so naturally as if on a brief
outing will never return.
Already they are lying
spilled in the road, their simplest
lantern or sandwich
an ancient mystery now
to us, who find the remains.
Was it these who, living,
created and handed down
all we know, bequeathed us
anxiety before the dead
silence, before the stare,
the sleep, the acquiescence,
the ill will and peace
of ruined objects that once
made perfect sense

to hands now stiff
and eyes that have surrendered
to the light? And when at last
we have reconstructed the whole site
as it must have been,
still nothing speaks. Were these
the first to take the wrong turning,
so that every later route
only strikes deeper
into the same sad country?

The Death of Francisco Franco

This is the bench where I wrote
the "Portrait of Francisco Franco." October 1975.
As Franco lay dying, clutching for death,
the impassive scientists in their unfelt fear
at this ending, gulf or bridge, trammelled him
in wires and tubes and held him back.
Franco. I showed him: man playing tennis
with a lice-ridden chicken for a ball.
I described how his nose was a gun
which he blew in the petals of his daughter.
And I prayed for his dying to last long.
In the tipping autumn this stone bench was cold
and the veering winds shook me.
How watery was the light, streaked
with palest yellow and blue, while the colours
of the bruise and of the wound mounted
in the struck trees. Tossing light:
an agitated water. Light shaken
when the wind would twist and release
the decimated branches. And the curled shreds,
the dispossessed, the leaves, were still supple
with an imitation life, the last of sap
caught in the cut-off veins. Lifted
from the ground or torn from boughs,
they eddied past me and dived in crowds,
shades of myth whirled by a last passion.

And the water in the sodden ground that seemed
to be rising in those rainless days
from a source in the earth—this moisture
was one with a moisture under my breast.

Some adolescent sadness had returned, a rising
of rain-fed waters. That noon of Franco's dying
echoed with a deserted evening that I felt
beneath my throat: a silent lake
devoid even of birds and singing insects.
Over it the sun is setting, and to its surface
rise patches of inflamed red and brownish purple,
as in the aftermath of a heavy blow.

But the frenzy all around, and within me
the stillness burning silently,
a spark in ash—
all this energy and agitation among ruins
seemed the commotion of a spring
rising in October in spite of reason
and the year's cycle. A human spring,
escaping only when deprivation
has stripped the husk away,
when there is nothing left of its old world
for the seed to eat. Touching the external,
the soil, the water, and the air, and feeling
above it through the mass the presence,
the possibility of light, it can begin at last
to augment itself and to live indeed.

So we look forward to winter. Prisoners
deprived of the world, we will march alone
surrounded by rifles, bootless in the snow,
with only some old rags tied over our feet,
or nothing. Life is locked up in ice around us,
all is veiled, all is chained, and many die.
But we walk on, happy for the blinding edge
where white and blue fit together;
and happy for the crumb that falls

into our vast hunger like one drop of rain,
a drop that is a seed self-watered. A seed
falls in the desert: seed of rivers and lakes,
of hushed voices in the air, of gentle darkness
that colonizes the brooding day, pays itself out
in dances and arabesques: shade of the troubled leaves
reincarnating a harsh ghost of light.
Perhaps nothing we knew will ever come again,
it is all destroyed, and these images...
nostalgia, this sound of water
that bubbles in the openings of our senses.
There is no water anymore,
this is not desert, the new man
is not a man, and has no body. Here there is only
loss, pain, and very seldom an ancient satisfaction
felt by one man, the only man,
on a blank background—
nothing, abstraction, the end of the physical world.
Yet here a promise touches that which was.
Here we know nothing, we touch some object beyond us,
or person it may be: someone else.
And in the total dark, total light, in the absence now
of all the soldiers, of snow, the locked earth, the heavens,
what is it that reminds us of a child
destroyed before it existed, child that we were.

That November Franco passed from death to death.
In life he was dust, and only the spit
of all good people
gave him weight and kept him on the earth,
stayed him in the real, prevented the wind
from carrying him off to the realm of pure cruelty.
In life he never awakened, but his snoring shadow
spread out over the world. There in Spain

they were covered by his anus and genitals:
an elephant hidden by a dime.
Here in America we were his left hand.
In his joints, conceived in arthritis,
cities and forests burned. How fat he was
in his polka-dot suit and tasselled hat,
surrounded by buck-toothed bald men even fatter:
so fat their legs could not reach the ground
and they rolled after him, grinning and picking up
the articles he kept dropping: dirty underclothes,
rusty popguns, eyeballs, and mangled coins.
And sometimes when he led them down a slope,
unable to stop they rolled over him,
crushing him into the mud and hurtling
to the bottom, colliding, rebounding,
gently settling into a drunken heap.

But was it his shadow over everything?
Or did his body become the world, in which men lived in caves,
eating acorns as in the golden age,
sleeping by their clubs, hating and desiring gold
that lit the domes of Franco's south,
founding the faith of perfect opposition?
For what were they to do, hidden on the hillsides
with ancient rifles, seeing day by day
the glittering patrols pass in steep valleys below?
Nothing but rock all around, bitter weeds
and a stunted cork tree, its sparse leaves blown
like the hair of an ancient, balding woman.
Crouching not to strike their heads on a sky
hard and bleached with the cold, they felt
neighbours of that unearthly point
where the wind was created, where some bitter spirit
flees downward from the world's crown

seeking the warm sound of palms, and a body
patient, inert, on a hilltop, late afternoon.
The wind seemed to them their desire. They were close
to some desire that was pure where all was cold,
bare, nearly invisible: a desire
that had scarcely any body
and yearned toward the south where Franco
tricked out his corpulence in fat commanders,
mitres, museums, women, the year of fashion,
the gestures of stone and oil. Desire
without a body: what can a ghost do
but howl and beat itself
against the wall of flesh, its tiny buffets
with no more power upon substance
than the tides of a reflecting pond
where the sun lies among long blades?
"Must the whole universe fall into ruin
before we can destroy this man?"

There on the porch of winter Franco died
and the leaves were driven around my ears
by a violence like spring's: strengthless shapes
carried past on the self-contradicting air,
savagely excited, starting in passion
and in passion turning back upon itself;
so clear that everything entered it, passed through it,
and it blew violently on all,
detaching fragments, bending, breaking,
furious and strengthless, destroying that which falls.
As if the bonds of slavery that hold
the beautiful surfaces together, the bodies
which create love, were broken and all the parts
were loosed onto currents, into confusion.
All that we hated, all that we opposed

is broken up. A winter-in-summer is ended,
summer of seductive ice, the fleshly glow
shining among reeds and green mounds,
and over the face of the strictest wall
a soft wind and birds in the blue-flowered vine.
O sack of corruptions: body that we loved,
falling apart, as a rotten mass in autumn
goes its separate ways on the stream,
or as ice shatters in spring.

In what false season did Franco seize
everything we had made and seem to take it
body and soul into his intestine? He drove you
far from Spain, your body, body of dreams,
Joan Miró, Benjamin Péret, Jorge Guillén;
and he drove many friends still farther,
till they were only shadows and words in light.
Then the cathedrals spit out jackals with whom
there is no argument, and from opened books,
from before the men and landscapes stretched to breaking
of El Greco, rose thick ghosts who stuttered and laughed,
leaving no room for men in Spain. Men fled
to dark corners, forgotten basements, wild hills:
the whole world to them became a cave
where no fire was lit by night, while the enemy
possessed the fields full of vines, the factories,
the day's light that draws redeeming colours
even from rubbish, and makes the least thing
strong. But did anything that these men said,
anything that I said, sitting here on this bench
in October 1975, persuade those hands
that reached at last through nature and bit by bit
tore Franco into death? Only our living,
which is the aging of the world, and was Franco's aging,

had that power. It released those winds
of late autumn, tugging at the last leaves,
the last scraps of flesh on the skeleton,
and today again those winds are loose,
the masts and rigging of the earth bared,
and the hulk rolls, the clouds that reveal
light continents are closing together, all colour
begins to resign itself to a steel-grey.
But let the hardness and the pain that comes
be a scalpel. Let the sharp edge
of blue wind on snow-encrusted field
cut Franco's rotting hands from the legacy.

It is the time when everything seems husk.
The love of one way, one summer though it betrayed,
asks hate for the hard season that approaches.
But winter light is the wildest, the calmest,
holding the most of ruin and exile
in the simplest look. And when the cold
has locked up all around us, we sit apart
in houses or walk in the false fading tropic
within our clothes, like a man in empty space.
We are cut off, gone out of things,
and we think our own thoughts,
free among the uncivilized powers,
examining a splendour, loose in a beauty
before all kindliness. That which we are
does not always upholster itself in comfort
or even life. And now the mind
falls crazily away from all it sees
and yet is rooted here, unmoving, pure
as the sky of this moment, incapable of change.
This falling which is buoyed up, this sureness
of death attended with the knowledge

that it can never come: this too is a summer,
summer of human things, where Franco's fleshy hand
turns to nothing as it gropes to seize
a conception. Here, in winter,
things grow to be no more than the bone of themselves,
and we will fall farther, to where the bone
and the bone's dust have never been: beyond,
exiled, outside of everything,
to the pith of earth's next summer
when the forms are given back,
when that which is meant is said.
The feathery leaves come out in the street
and among them the lamps light
of their own accord. And men return
to monuments that begin to move,
to a deserted city intact, to empty land
already staked out in farms, where Franco
is a dried leaf that blows away.

What They Prayed For

What they prayed for seemed not much,
and already, despite the dusty weeds
extending to the sky, a possession:
a grassy land, lightly wooded,
rolling, with intricate slopes
and crossed by streams, relieved
by lakes, pools, and reedy swamps.
Breezes over the water to suggest
music; and, visible from rises,
the ocean, glinting among the trees,
near so that when you are silent
within yourself it can be heard.
Also shade and shadow:
an openness to the sun,
to the sky, that is yet defended
and moistened by fingers of the earth.
Then a few things will follow
from these first conditions: women
singing in full light and at dusk
before reflecting water;
and some way to live together
that is not a scandal and a shame.

Music and Exile

You are the only tenant who never leaves
that hotel forgotten in the hills
that I love and visit at all seasons:
muddy spring, summer of drenched crops,
autumns and winters veiled in rain.
There some disease working from underground
has changed to purple the huge fleshy trees.
And there you come down the steps, wander the halls
among the political refugees
who live there briefly, always flowing through.
You never join them at the sleeted windows
where they stand looking out nervously
along the road, expecting the police.
In the evenings you weave through them in the bar
while they play chess and cards
and ceaselessly form governments in exile,
and it makes you smile faintly to hear
their harmless manifestos.
Your thoughts turn to the women in rooms above
with children as white as worms,
young wives whose flesh quickly grows grey.
It's as if they are falling into dust
here while they linger in life
thinking of gardens around their parents' homes.
And in imagination, imagination alone,
you place a light hand on the children's heads
because they never play
and they look at you with the same knowledge
that visited your girlhood.
Yet they are even without your desperation,

your power to be drunk with defeat and memory.
You think of fires never built in the snow.

Some say that mine is a work of images
appearing and ceasing to exist in succession,
like static and silence on a radio tuned at night
to some station perhaps beyond its range:
there is only nothingness to connect the flashes.
How is it that no one has detected you,
your voice, the thread of all things seen and heard?
Is it that you are not an image
but a ghost, the idea of a melody,
a cry from beyond the loud wall of the rain?

The thunderstorm lights up this inn almost in ruins.
The sky is a huge man
whose blood is on fire.
All night, one after another, the sections
of his network of veins explode:
for a second we see the jagged paths
cut off at their ends
fading in cloud.
The storm casts an intermittent gleam
on the inn where the lights have flickered and gone out.
Now and then the lightning picks out the faces
in a glow of gold and thick red.
Sometimes a few words are exchanged in darkness.
One hopes to obtain false papers.
One plans again the murder
of the officer who tortured his wife to death:
but that was fifty years ago
on the edge of Asia,
and the officer must be dead in the war

or of some disease
or peacefully, covered with honours, among his children.

The chess game continues in the dark
in their huge memories distended by idleness,
and the flashes give time to make a move
that already they have meditated for ages:
always the same adversary,
the same losses and gains.

And you:
you know that there is nothing within their power,
not even the coils of rope and the pistols
that some have hidden in their rooms:
occasionally there is suicide
but another always comes and fills the place.
Now, oppressed by the storm passing swiftly over,
they are thinking of the locked borders,
of freedom in the mountains,
and they don't see you pacing in and out among them.
But I hear you, I hear the rustle of your dress
and I know you love me.
I wish I could awaken and find you with me.
Softly you are speaking to yourself, to me,
and now I can almost see you
where you sit unnoticed at a dirty table
in the darkness shuffling, reshuffling the tattered cards.

Views

This huge tree: sleeping
against its trunk, we thought
the stars were its distant berries,
the sky its foliage, the sun and moon
a pair of mating birds
who wove a monotonous chase
of courtship through its limbs.
Sleeping, we thought the claw of its root
clutched the shreds of a torn
idea, gathered them in a ball
and made continents, gave form
to a grateful remnant of water
beating, bodiless fists,
at the walls of wall-lessness.

One coming upon our bodies
as we dreamed there
in spring found them green,
hard, bitter. In summer, returning,
found them too beautiful to touch,
at morning and evening
covered with cool, fresh tears.
In autumn they seemed to him soft,
brown with irresolution,
in the act of deciding like penitents
to give themselves back.
In winter he found nothing
but a hallucination of two lovers
in the snow in the zero weather
twining in a shell
of their own light, naked

and unbothered, cold as the cold,
like stars fallen on earth
in the spot where we had been.

Next spring, two small forms appeared
near our places, and while these
were not ourselves, to the watcher
it made small difference—he praised
some shadow of us and them.
So the air shook with fear,
or was it anger? Night
became unreal. We awoke.

Now, in the day, with what
care we treasure the dream.
Of that tree, we make our tongue.
The voiceless sky we call
our skull, and to night's silent thoughts,
frozen and distant, we give words.
We rest, enjoying the watcher
as we recall him, his puzzlement
and sadness at our slow passing,
his horror at the pure winter glare
of blessedness where we withdrew
and apparitions followed.
We love his speechless
pleasure at spring and the forms
which return, in which he loves us.
But we do not return.
All this we recall while outward
our eyes are opening
into a city of mere light.

Prayer for Prophecy

May the old women of music, frozen
in days before memory into words
(they cooled and suffered into use
between anvil and hammer), give
my ear a rumour of why the stars
flee and in what directions. Not
how the atoms and the grids of force
assembled like network the inept
sprawling design, but the future,
for which the loose lip of the sea
drools on this beach, sucking down
the dissolving sand. To what
purpose each winter the moaning chords
of night drag out their limp tails
longer, and with reptilian stares
rekindle soot in the day's face.
And if to this depth of nature I
am not destined to reach, then let
the country and the streams of water
that freshen valleys content me, hiding
in their sluggish harmony the cold
springs of the blood that clogs my heart.

The Beginning

Struck by the sun, I thought if everything burned and was forgotten
we would produce it all from the earth.
From freshness, from cleanness.
Across waving grasses that concealed no ruins
it would be a million years before Gilgamesh went seeking
beyond mountains and under rivers the survivor of the flood.
Would we attempt and always fail to surprise an unknown one
who walks in a garden, tending the pear trees?
There would be no stories yet, only amazement—
though we must notice soon that earth, the varieties of men and times,
are not inexhaustible, and days repeat:
even days before any creature has yet died.
But think of our feet on a soil in which no fathers lie.
Of the first to find his wife beside him, stiff, eyes open,
staring fixedly at the morning. And of that one who discovers
the skin may be torn from the living body, and beneath
is a fresh landscape of red and grey, streams and winding caves,
riven terrain of moving valleys and soft mountains.
Would he who committed the first simple murder be shown in waking
     dreams
the infinite length of the tradition he had founded?
To console his sleeplessness, would he travel and come
to plains of frost and establish peoples forever
dependent on artificial fire?
And perhaps no law created what has been,
but some chance error: standing on ground burnt clean
by bombs, we might not stumble again: now
there would be other actions, and so other visions, explanations.
Yet say it were all repeated, the same pain, by will or need.
Still, to be the first—the first to wander,
so that no movement could ever be made by men

that had not already been ours: no ascent or decline,
no speech with another, no account of heaven or the atmosphere,
no taming of flocks, building of ships, invention of bread.
It is our word for desert, mountain, river,
they will seek forever in their many words.
Through the multiplication of their bodies and acts, they grope
as through shadows for our body struck by the sun.

You, Whoever You Are

1

Fable of isolation and violence,
a man
where the crickets speak
to winter's open mouth:
the shadow of a nail
crawls among ripe blackberries,
their vines that bind and tear
swift feet. And soft
as breath at the closing
of a quiet sentence,
the September evening fills
with sickles, curved silhouettes
that fall toward the tangled
bank of the river. Your hand
falls over his, your palm,
cold from holding and offering
the violet air. And if a thought
desperate at the cranes returning
to their base in the shadows
blazes in him, this you harbour too
under cooling hills, as your molten
gold robed the breasts of trees
and a burning monster all day.

2

In you dark odours
and a sound of moisture and wind
flower, bringing to light

flesh that is the choired heads
of the grasses, the linked
fingers of numberless trees.

Is it solved in you, the desolating
scent of the uncovered ground?
The constant and sleep-denying rain
reveals an unquiet darkness,
water fleeing through the wrinkles
in yellow mud.

And the monotonous music of it prays
to you as to those powers
that have made life
interminable and too brief.

3

You too, fumbling here
with your hand that never closes.
Your isolation, hour of figures
cut from a spectrum in air,
crossing your palm, an expedition
of souls unborn. You watch,
your request limp on the slopes,
the bleaching sky, dark places
where a bride's moisture evaporates.
In a wooden house, all doors
and shutters open,
at times thrashing in a gust,
someone sits upright sleeping. Things
drift in his hand
under the avalanche of shadows.

4

Helpless in the amber and sleep
of your still life, you stir:
high leaves
in a wind that does not touch the ground,
or thistle exploding into flax.
But these things are your thought,
these and the mating butterflies
which pass so close to the sleeper's ear
that the sound of their wings brushing together
wakes him. How compare you
to your own thought? You sing
inwardly, struck by the sun,
meditate under grey sky, dream
in the moon's phases, let all things
sink back into strengthless memory
in the dark of the moon.
Never in its profusion
does your thought reach beyond itself.
Even the gesture of defiance, the leafless
tree gnarled like a fist thrust up
from a grave, rests perfectly within
its form of death. And our eyes
return effort to this stillness,
and to the living forms a desire
to burst the bounds of growth.
Our eyes: poor shoots
of the human seed, that old idea you had
to gather all in one reflection
with power to detach itself from the mirror
and live, and move, elsewhere.
Still you lie like a man and woman
in adjacent rooms. The heat

rises from the beds
and a hand seems hidden in the dark air
ready to appear and bless.
In the mind of each, all beauty
lies behind some door,
all emptiness is here. The trembling
of a paralysis, your drying
grass blades vibrate in place,
your birds move, either at random
or directed by pure need,
and some emblem of motion sleeps
in every fact of stillness.

5

After a fissure of sunlight
we spent ten years
walking among your dead
in the stone wind,
your amber breath
which their motions
turned grey. But even there
the blinded wall still ran
with vines and tongues.
In that weighted cloister
under the tattered ceiling
that sagged lower, no tendril
came to curl its light shade
on naked foreheads:
a night of oil
thickening in its swell.
But even so in a clearing
was a landing where we met
the lightest boat

and were carried onto the still river.
And below us a blue face
now and then would break
the mirror of black water.

6

In the scent of clover and hay,
in the pleasure of wild heat
subdued, a wet shade extracted out of fire
where the forest is crumbled
and drawn up again by light,

in all things most impervious
to the transmutation of thought
that falls in you, a hand
feeling darkly for an absent tool,

you meditate your aggression,
anarchy and silence. You hide your face
whose expression is peace
reflected from the sea that rolls and rots
a lost acorn cup, the ship of discoverers
offshore of a new world
where the trees appear far off as flames of green water,
and where men's thoughts, ashore already,
are finding out tobacco and gold.

And sometimes you attack,
you rush out from every barrier
like a flood in a dream
where the furniture, the walls and floors
burst up, are water,
and startled the dreamer wakes

to the dry room, the bed
silent, not to affirm or to deny
that it is a ship of water
bearing a spirit of water
in the forms of the sea.

7

The lover is a dream you have.
Born of your brain, he strayed
through the things that happen there,
learning rhythms, expectancy,
and a pitiful few masks of the spring,
a few words of all
that winter, autumn, and summer have to say.
In everything there were traces of your body,
as a voice heard
is the trace of an unseen speaker;
and he saw hands emerge,
one from the north, one from the south,
and exchange a sealed letter.
Why was there no one beside him?
So in your dream the lover
split himself in two
and the part that loved you
hated and wed the part
that took your place. You dreamed
that yet he would be born
and lie beside you. In your sleep,
in your dreams he cried out alone,
because you are the only other
and he is lost in you.

8

Why, if you have hidden from me,
do you linger where light
moulds itself on green fingers,
on tattered hands
shading the tombs from the blaze
that denies all mercy, cutting out
the inscriptions and the drying grass?

Here you seem to walk.
I glimpse a flank, a stream
of hair turned green in the shadow,
passing between two stems—
you, or your image, pierced
by low fluttering notes.
And it seems possible: the legend
of water walking in human form
the waves of dust. You passed
almost unseen, but suddenly
the thought of death
was filled with a knowledge
of ghosts returning to bodies gnawed
for eons by greedy salt.
And my words, spoken
in anger and misery against men
who kill themselves with eyes open,
passed into your eyes
truly open, and returned to my mouth
as this air: milk of your breast.

9

Your voice:
first sign among dreamed remains
(shattered spectral walls obscuring
the city of perfected stone)
that images are of our eyes.

In it all history
was contradicted. Human, it called
for a being that moved, invisible
within the light, to intervene.
At dawn it muttered to slow worms
grazing on utter dark.

In sand moistened by the water's lip
was the root that, smothering,
clutches the murderer and cries...

your voice: desire.
And this alone distinguished you
from chill evenings at summer's ending,
from the earth.

10

Sometimes I imagine a crying face
dissolved above me...not in the rain
but in the hardest crystal,
the ruthless transparency that gives
the colour of cold
to the purest light we know. No moisture
(dew or the rivers or storm)
is its crying, only the blankness among things:

the silence not of words unspoken
but of words unknown, the forms
curled on themselves in a necessary dream.

And its crying burns, self-fed,
in all the tongues for whom a single leap
is at once body and death.
A flash: one dies and another rises,
smaller, more distant, cool.
They are thrown back from their perimeters,
huddle together in the deepening walls
of charcoal. They have said almost nothing:
only a brittle complaint, a low insistence
snapping twigs, exploding the moist pebbles.
Yet already, under wet boughs, hissing
in green night, only a buried glow remains:
as if left for chance travellers to find
here, in the deaf music of the frogs.

11

Stay where you are, don't fly
still deeper in the self-absorption
of your wing, last livid shape
afloat on the wood's scaffold.
The fog that muffled
in cool mornings the river's warm
and almost silent throat
is removed now, burned
by the hand that sharpens apples
and mummifies the ones not eaten.
Now the glow that arouses pain
and brings it to such intensity that it dies
cracks the shield of its rusted lantern:

at last nothing is shaded
from the paleness it projects.
What is this white shell,
that the silent colours hurry to speak themselves
into its static curvings,
its diminished spectrum, shades of milk?
And will go on speaking despite
immobility, deafness, an absent bird
that broods over the ash.

12

Life you held on the palm
of your extended hand.
Why could our hands not close upon it?

Your gaze fell on us
from beyond a tangled curtain,
the yellow withes of the willow
trailing yellow leaves, from which we peered.
In the stream we glimpsed the reflection of an eye,
a glance setting fire to the ripples,
making things burst from themselves
as the flax bursts from the pods
which yet are motionless: it merely appears,
as the eye suddenly will pick out
a brilliant jay, frozen, watching in the vines.

And so to dusk, gradually assembling its dark empty bridge
into the heart of each thing.
And so to stillness, the end of us
travellers: children
who had now arrived and been annulled.
Yet out of that silence

and the place where there is no motion but communion
nevertheless anguish gathered itself, proceeded:

soon adult voices would shout our names, summoning.
Dinner would be ready,
although we had never been less hungry.

13

Always opening and closing,
your light sometimes a wall,
sometimes an eye, your air
either distance or a hand...
The birches filled with chaos
can mutter aloof, collecting
sparks without meaning,
pure instances of you.
Or in a corridor bees pass
and from high among drying needles
a brilliant dime
glazes the surface.
The greeting still returns
from vegetable words
to cellars where wings are a badge of foolishness
and the only tongue is human.
Among your stems, these leavings
half reclaimed by the rain and mud:
bottles, cigarettes, soaked papers,
photographs of women that someone pierced
with arrows and holes. On your path
so full of fluid openings
that inspire the light, this evidence
of a being to which everything is sealed.

14

When we wanted never to sleep again,
you brought us back
from the riot of unassembled blocks,
and every face that drew itself
on the black slate
of a doorless doorway.

Even the gnats
that burned their rootless schema above the path
rested in your eye.
A glance threaded the stems,
an arch opened
on the sky over a cemetery,
we were shown and we forgot
so many details of strange flesh
nervously bared and offered,
the way a cloud forgets its form.

Also we stumbled on heavy clouds
caught in shapes and fallen in wild wheat:
stones of an ancient wall
that once had lain on one another
without the aid of mortar.
In the afternoon
you withdrew them from your moist shadow.

15

Your high burials, your baths
made by a persistent torch
from the ruin of water,
your haze of curtains

burning and opening
on richer curtains —

a hand's attempts
to wipe the mist from the encrusted
window or mirror.

Why do you return so often
to this season that repays you
with dying, your own penny
tarnished with jealousy?
In the torrent you
are only a tiny raft,
a few saplings woven together,
still green, unaware you are dead, dragged
with chains to the empty sea.

Yet you admire the artistry
of the flood: a rock
worried to a statue of cancer,
a dwindling tower whose gaze
pursues a pheasant in the burning woods.
Even these, which a god would call
shapes of death, you hoard
in your sealed vault with each smallest
detail that crumbles from a life.

16

Abandoned, you return
to the place of the last meeting. Dying,
you summon a more than natural strength,
again compose yourself
to the beauty that was yours before the illness spoke,

before the betraying depths declared themselves
to the surface, to translucent skin,
the face that colours now
alternately with peace and desperation.

And all that is known of you,
the downward path, the unseen locust seized
in the midst of its chirring by a wasp,
the stars fleeing from every point,
the crimes committed at every point,

gathers in this last offering
you never refuse to make.
Still held and framed
in a vessel that vanished long ago,
let it gleam there, a shape of water,
a shape of clear sap and of blood
faintly reflecting our drying faces,
in every form of yours poised at our lips.

PART II

1986–1994

The Tradition

I think we are the heirs of slaves,
a race of water bearers to the patient herd.

But whose memory reaches so far back?
We can see how quickly the children of our day
forget the names of their parents newly dead.
No documents are found in our houses.
No object we make will last two generations.
No skills are handed down
but how to live each day with the flies, the wind
that veers and whips the dust ever replenished,
and distant shouting, random sirens at night.

In these sheds between compulsive howl and silence,
between young and old, what knowledge falls?
Now and again some few among our proverbs
are shown by science to be not wholly meaningless.
Our habits bear resemblance to religion,
our jokes to story. Scholars discuss our culture,
whether vestigial or primitive;
whether by instinct or tradition we patch
hovels of newspaper, boxes, corroded tin
in barren lots sown with splinters of bricks;
whether there is some reason in our claim
that a calm word from this or that deathbed
has exalted starvation, typhus, and mute lethargy.
Our only leisure, afforded by long moments
straining with constricted bowels, gives rise
to pride in our own penetration,
our contempt of self-denial, our ignorance of pleasure.

More than any future,
we want the past to have been marvellous.
Ancestors: these are our one invention.
Pirates, smugglers, revolutionaries.
Beachcombers piling shells, staring over the sea.
Magi of forgotten disciplines,
the content of their researches beyond us —
although the banal formulas that survive
are full of implication.

And the real fathers?
Those who in fact dropped sperm in broken cisterns,
moaning to create us? There is no way to know them,
unless to presume that they were much like us.
Then, at times, they too
felt themselves cherishers of the fire that hides,
inscribes itself only in ash, and like some toad
endures centuries in a toppled well,
sleeping under the rim stones with their forgotten script.
On clear nights in the lanes of the warehouse district,
they too must have glimpsed the setting moon —
its blurred figures buried in watery light —
and claimed it theirs, as the only beings
still conscious in that place and at that hour.

The Explorer

Here among the forks and plates
they want me to remember and describe.

I remember this much:
there weren't any words in the white deserts, skies, and tombs,
no words in the north,
only green empty air, black limbs, low grey rock
by planes of steely water, and ice in shadows.

Since I came back, all of the words I know
have been wandering in me among those remembered things.
Never yet has one word found a place,
not even a tree or a profile in a cliff
to stop at, to remind it of why it came.

Despite the winds that blow there,
I can still hear the questions.
To appease these talkers I would almost tell them
how quiet I am in those places.
I wander there, small and alone,
and everything seems familiar, a part or power of myself,
yet nothing recognizes me.
And if I stayed, nothing would save my life.

Even now, while my hand lies with stainless steel and glass,
my feet are in the sand or snow,
huge cliffs or flats around me, always the huge sky,
and they are in me as I'm in them.

But I can't reach or touch them.
I never can enter them deeply enough

or take them far enough down into me.
So much love, such hunger: I've brought back nothing else
and this failure, wonder, silence is my life.

The Painter

Is life wasted staring over the sea?
This is the way I worship the beachcomber god,
lord of driftwood that has wandered for years
to stop now at my feet. I stare,
for what is there to see? At night
only twelve animals that foolishness
places among the stars. This life
wants no place in their wheel: it flashes
once from the earth, a fish leaping,
and vanishes. By day I see shacks and trees,
the burning paleness between ocean and sky,
thin, almost absent shades of violet,
one part murex in a million parts of brine:
sustaining light, the painter's element,
pastel, pale to the point of non-existence.

Stare at the sea, choke
in the dusty power the sun has over it.
Liquid desert. Theatre of hallucination.
Whoever goes there will see what may be seen:
men with the heads of birds, men with noses
that are long spatulas for taking bread from the oven,
men with one eye, one ear, one arm,
one buttock, one testicle: they hop over the waves.
Look. But let the desert saints
go first, encounter, clear away
all things that laugh at travellers through the waste,
the blank of water, life's source.

They say the devil comes there
in the form of a beautiful woman

to tempt men from their vows. I too desire
love, which is not proper to this life.
Here naked women—not anything in woman's form,
but women—pass on the beach all day. For most
I am too sick, but sometimes one will take me,
and such...they love my room
filled up with canvases,
the sound of my warped guitar, the slosh of gin.
This is what I am. They love
some aggregate of ocean sunsets,
the mood of pleasure pitted against time,
of idleness and resolute decay.
Nothing, sentiment, a minor chord
as crabs skitter in the crimson sheen
of wet sand at evening and morning.

Day by day this path up and down my beach,
this daubing at starfish, sandshrubs, driftwood,
and all the wreckage of intimate disaster
washed here from the hotels or overseas.
A high-heeled shoe, a spar, a nylon, tangle together
in webs of kelp. The paint on the canvas
sags, boneless, tending to shades of weed
and oily sand. Only the blue
that needs no form is brilliant, clear,
and sends its splendour down lanes through the leaning shacks
and in the rotting forest. The moment captured here
sufficed, suffices, for itself, but not for me.
And I reject labour too, and am rejected.

This loud rhythm of silence, baffling glare,
this gaze of the horizon that sees all.
Is life wasted staring over the sea?
I have been here, my feet planted in sand

among the trees dropping limp chains of white flowers,
flashes off lacquered leaves, the twinkling destruction
of green in pure light...I have been here...
Is it spring? So many seeds are drifting,
it must be spring. But I have been here
all of a summer that never had a beginning.
Or it began, and ended, and I forget,
confused by the drooping ropes of petals
like strings of fishes caught and hung in the air.

Lament of a Hunter

In the halls and escalators of this castle
and sealed in its dungeons: the desiccating
sunlight that never clouds. The open-concept
spaces that curl on a green plain down
to watering places, lakes captured in crystal bulbs...
A mailed and greaved and mounted man,
or a naked runner with a spear, I course
the boundaries of the desk-top farms and curse
chicken wire, domestic swine, sheep filling narrow tracks.

Faith is this wandering in the parks that kindness
has set aside as if I were trailing the caribou
as when twice each year they used to cross our barrens. Sorrow
is these women who may praise magnificence
rarely, talking in their sound sleep, but take
not one who passes in a day or a week,
with the game or the wars, but the man who dies
as they do, imperceptibly, through years.

Violins have driven the monkeys' mockery and flight
from the forest of white, straight, branchless trunks.
Perpetually in training for nothing under the sun,
my chest swells and gleams as Hector's never did.
With the tattoo needle I draw caste and blood.
By night through clothes I have carefully clawed to a shred,
my nipples point like darts. And for a shield
in the back alleys I bang the trashcan lid.

Again

The strap of one of your silver shoes is broken.
Our little fire kicks in the dry twigs.
Blood describes a natural jagged curve
where a tree drew a nail across your fleeing breast.

A juiceless orange looms through heavy leaves:
on the plain out there the city is eating itself
like radium, iron, the sun — or like a bone
that outlives its body and becomes a club.

There are compensations in being the last remnant.
For instance this pause, our bodies fitted warmly
into dusk's patient movement.
Here in a darkness new to us
but also not unremembered, we feel
a star coming to claim each dying friend,
coming softly, to the navel retying a cord
cut long ago
in an hour of pain that returns.

One in delirium speaks of the dark bar
with vomit on the floor where we were laughing
when the warning came, and a story starts to grow:
"Remember that mirrored ballroom by the river
starred below us with images of our candles..."

Soon we will bury the image of what we were,
how once we swayed in currents, in mass assemblies,
the vain panic of crowds that, always growing, dwindled
to tribes without memory, without earth.
Only some shreds recur.

You're nobody's sweetheart now, one whistles.
His blood escapes
through the bandage you made from your gold bodice:
hard nylon, sequins adoring the moon.

The Signs

Whenever we prayed for a sign, someone saw it in the sky.
Whenever we prayed for a word, someone heard voices.
These visitations always came to people far off in the provinces.
Suspiciously we listened to the garbled accounts,
too beautiful, too much like well-beloved old legends.

We did not believe in signs
and yet we never stopped praying for them.
Then simple people began to see silver ships in the clouds
and animals unknown to science
prowling upright like men through suburbs and vestigial forests.

Praying tortured us.
Night and day our thoughts could not stop asking
for earth to be founded anew, established in perfection,
for pleasure in the heart of danger, attainment in rest,
for things we could not imagine or conceive.
We felt the years slip by in prayer
as if in fever,
unable to pause and think and solve our lives,
to speak to the women who left us for others,
to understand how much we had wanted from them
and how much more they had longed to give.
Arthritis was sealing up even our jaws.
Dreams never brought any more assurance that all is well.

But we understood finally what the wise man prays for:
not to see any sign.
Not to meet the Buddha or the Sphinx
or any monster on the road.
Not to be struck with lightning

and be made forever, only, the one who saw the sign.
The wise man prays to be left alone by vision
with his books and instruments, to consider
how dawn enlightens treetops and night the stars.

The Boy

Sometimes a man feels a boy walk out of him
and close the door. Then, turning to a window,
the man can watch him, always growing smaller,
a long way down the path that gently drops
across the steep hill. He's walking into the sea,
a white and yellow sea: a spray of goldenrod
splashes his thigh, the froth of Queen Anne's Lace
and flax from pods bursting wavers, twists, unravels.
He's going down there, going back, to the core
and thread of water, a stream flowing within
the ocean of things, still fresh with that final freshness
that is warm when a boy is sad, cool when he's tired.
He's going to fish there, alone all day, with his hands.
And it doesn't matter that he won't catch anything,
when the sun sets he goes home.

Days Along the Banks

Sometimes the dead return of their own accord
with all the mingled scents and seeds in the air
along these paths they used to know,
effaced now by roadbuilders,
strewn with machines and heaps of materials.

Or else a glint, when morning air
breaches the curtains, will stir closed eyes
and a screen is torn away:
there, surprised and angry, still muttering
their old plans, are the dead. They sit
in their rooms of which two walls were never completed.
Their chairs face the southern fields
littered with browning corn unreaped.
Crowds of blackbirds—the small flames
flashing on bituminous wings—
wheel above rusted threshers.

The dead are still suffering their final illness,
and at dusk the shadow of a doctor who never arrives
falls across them. Growing restless,
they take you out to walk in the last light.
The summer evening is hot
and they must move slowly, the heart is still diseased.
All the dogs and children greet them
and they know the name of every plant.
They gather mushrooms, repeating botanical terms,
and never falter in picking those most healthful,
leaving the poisonous to flourish undisturbed.

At the end of every lane they pass is the river.
Their way through spacious night is marked out
by fireflies under willows.
The dead talk of days along the banks,
strong days of continuous rhythm and always new melody
linking your childhood to theirs.

They talk, but nothing matters to them now,
not even their own sadness at their failures
and the things that chance disallowed.
Not death, which continues to overtake them.
Not you, who will awaken in love again,
confused, forgetful, glad,
believing they are returned.

Putting Up for the Night

They put me under the eaves. The rain keeps waking me,
beating through this dreary thaw, breaking up
the ice on the roof. I hear it shift and slide
and wonder: Did I come here along a drowning
highway, slashed with streaked reflections,
scribbled ledgers and crushed suits
in the seat behind me, arriving as always after midnight
at this same motel? Or on a worn-out donkey
that struggled almightily to draw each hoof
out of the sucking mud, with only a few
onions left in my saddlebags, to a smoky inn?

It scarcely matters. The mutter of low talk
comes through from the next room, laughter and swearing
rise up at times, my sill is etched
in a thin line of light, now and again
without rhythm but without ceasing
someone opens a distant door and staggers
along the hallway, falling against the wall
outside my room, pausing to lean there
as the storm lashes out, renewed...eternal things,
the sounds of vomit, liquor, urine
mixing with the rain.

The first time I woke up
the wind had died, a soft patient rain
brushed the walls more quietly than silence,
more everlastingly. I saw, between two floods of sleep
from an instant of utter waking,
no harm in the world. No harm could come to me.

Whatever pain might break or rot my body,
whatever might be lost, it was all there
in a peace with which I encompassed everything,
all the sorrow of
life, this childish moment of blindness.
Why did I ever go to sleep again?
But it seemed then that nothing could ever change
and sleep was my blessing. The second time I woke,
the building shook under the wind's hammer.
I knew at once that all was ruined.
How did it happen that I was merged
with these fragile tendril arms, this head on a thin neck,
and suffered for them, and would suffer much more
when they will be crushed or lopped like worms?
How could it be that I was so old and still withering
and if I cried out, no matter if I screamed and screamed,
no one would come, nothing would stop my going
and give me back childhood and joy?

How could I ever go to sleep again?
But horror changed shape, was unconsciousness
until this hour, the final waking.
Dawn's grey ooze silts up the room,
the coughing, slamming of doors, shouts
and distant noises, horses whinnying, engines grinding,
the restlessness that signals rest is over
until another day has finished with the body.

You who brought me here, leave me,
don't drive me out, don't fill my head to overflowing
with aches, my guts with the waste of night
and new desires. You—power, fate, or impotent
sameness of every road—let me lie here awhile:

soon enough I'll see the stable yard outside
or a cracked swimming pool, and know again
what I am, and what I have to do.

Pandora's Box

At the end of *Pandora's Box*, the film by Pabst,
the cravings of Lulu the nymphomaniac are finally to be fulfilled:
Jack the Ripper approaches Lulu's place as a fog
covers the camera eye. We know that under it
a love too sublime to be exhausted
is more than satisfying dark-eyed Lulu.
In his fury to be disburdened,
he is opening new vulvas in her back, sides, arms,
especially in her throat,
until she is all one openness, one sigh, one stillness.

These two are consumed by love, murdering
and dying at the root of my tongue all day.
No one can love as much or sleep as long
as Lulu desires, and her desperation
makes the hollow air above the earth still emptier
and fills it with forms like rags
all flying in a wind that streams to the vacuum.
No one can absorb the fierce passion of Jack
impatient of sex, its slow limited ecstasy
leading only to a revelation that cannot be seized,
or even remembered: a dream
that presumably one dreamed during a dreamless night.
The knife, which reveals strange things,
is the key to their needs: they are looking
for the gold in time, in the smooth drift of the flesh.
And already it has unlocked convolutions that make the sky
    seem simple,
bowels darker, more twisted than the depths of the soil,
fluids that congeal in the air more eagerly than lava,
a heart that stops so soon, the swift years seem long.

Dead, or waiting as still as death in desire,
Lulu's body holds history in a nutshell.
First it is one body.
Then it is seized by love,
revealed as many bodies, and dispersed.
It has its brief fiery phase,
its gelatinous phase,
its cooling phase while it pullulates with tiny lives,
its phase of dust and then the wind blows it away.
The wind blows it away, and look—there is no gold.
But a grizzled prospector,
squatting, hunched, still sifts through Lulu's bones:
it must be here, for long ago
she stole all that was promised—this is why he loved her.
Or maybe this was not she, but another: she is elsewhere.
So he cleans his tools and sets out again,
dwindling, dissolving into the water-burdened air:
Jack the Ripper approaches Lulu's place as a fog...

Mahler Symphony No. 4 on the Record Player

Something vast but small is happening there
in the corner of the room, where it's dark.
The man in lamplight can hear it
across huge distances of carpet
and the clamour of his book.

Triremes are laying down Greek fire
and the shouts of sea-borne crowds, dying, come over the water.
Above that fight, in orange smoke, the human cries
are drowned in a goddess's swelling voice
as the bodies drown in the ocean.

Also a man with a cane is struggling through a thicket
and sees a wild boar coming toward him
here where no animal but the dog or squirrel has been seen
    for a century.
And he knows at once what it means,
that the moment of fear and the moment of salvation are one.
Up ahead the animals are swarming,
every kind of animal and every plant
since the first cell, all the ideas
of fish and fungi, and to every form its own colours.
Some obscure struggle is going on
but nothing is obscured: each figure is firm and complete.
At the height of each of the day's seasons—
morning, the afternoon, evening, and night—
the whole landscape and its labour
peels like a film from earth and rises, disappearing,
leaving behind a clearer version of itself.

It ends. The man turns it back
to its beginning.
Again the wanderer wanders at his leisure
at peace or dissolved in nightmare.
The gods, soldiers, machines, and animals
are crying out again:
something about the power
who created them and put them there
in that steep black fosse that winds in and in.
Something about the power who owns them,
to whom they seem vaguely different, new,
each time he makes them repeat their lives exactly.

Orpheus in Ontario

On a stone made blinding white by August sunlight
roaring silently in a dry place among the pine trees,
the man still has about him the smell of earth and damp.

His loose robe, his ancient instrument
don't offend here, where nothing's out of place or time
and old fashions are often suffered to survive.

And if you seem to see the bluejays,
cardinals, goldfinches, the squirrels and woodpeckers,
groundhogs and field mice dancing when he plays,

you're free to think it's nothing but the patter
of the wood's business resuming, as it always resumes
when any man barges in here but then sits down a while

and is still. Maybe the dancing of the trees
is only light wind in the branches making a rhythm
of moving shade and the sound of pine cones dropping.

And his playing, a music that isn't music
but one long varying chord—maybe the air
and not his fingers moves among those strings.

A fever's in this air. Summer is old,
so old its wrinkling skin is almost ready
to flare up in the heat and burn off.

But now this older man, or something, the wind, recalls
coolness, darkness, water and its wandering sound,
how it leaps up sometimes in a dry space near a rock

to the surface, gleams, and magnifies the sun
but dwindles, with its orderless shreds of song,
from the river it left behind it in the earth.

Kingdom and Empire

In the garbage and trampled leavings of the empire
we remember the Good Kings.

How great and small they were, like children,
on their tiny hillside that seemed vast to them,
as to children a street with a few houses
beside a brook and a last stand of trees
is vast. Their kingdom: such clashes of great armies,
fear, deadly intrigue, ruined hope,
such tortuous intercourse with gods,
so many songs, so many intricate
rites of appeasement at burial, bed, and table,
and still such pleasure...
We dreamed but never thought how it was all
a kingdom of thought and dreams.

                              And then
the dreaming world rolled over in its sleep
and the scene changed. From a place deep within
rose the desire for conquest against death,
unity among the things of this world,
empire. And that is how we came to be
believers, soldiers. We crossed the Alps
and stood behind great Caesar, swords in our hands
and at our feet corpses of those wild men
who would not submit, and who had killed so many
out of the pure exuberance of their strength.

Petra

The city, recently abandoned when we arrived,
was as disappointing as usual with legendary sites.
Nothing of labyrinth in the grid of the few streets.
Nothing of garden in the dusty acacias along gravel paths.
True, it was a city of rose-coloured stone.
But only as others are cities of tarpaper or corrugated tin.

No place is totally devoid of wonders.
We found a statue of their god:
a young woman, lithe and tall, an athlete.
All her internal organs were carved as hanging down her breast
from her teeth clenched on the trachea.
Her expression was anguish at seeing what should not be seen.
An elegant gesture of her two hands indicated heaven and earth.
Her flawless, expressionless back and hips, however,
were still capable of inspiring lust,
if there were one to feel it.

After a few months we had lived our fill in every house and room.
We knew each photograph, each letter,
all the hidden treasures of pornography,
old uniforms and toys in attics,
cellars piled with the tools of a people that doesn't need to work.

True, the city was half as old as time: much had gone on.
Experts might keep themselves busy there for years.
But we already knew all about the ones who lived there.
How their pleasures ceased to move them,
yet they found themselves unable to change at all,
afraid to give up or alter a single gesture.
Then one day they set out, taking everything with them,

to see if there were other people with another love;
or at least a new colour of skin, a strange caress.

Aeneas

A boy, I was hidden from myself in a thick cloud.
No one could see or touch me
and I went among men unhindered,
without being asked my nation or why I'd come.

I went through the city and saw it was all made new.
No place was closed to me, not the councils, the worksites,
the women's chambers, the palace of the queen.
Whatever people were doing—scooping muck to deepen the harbour,
sighting the outline of a theatre and marking it with string,
quarrying titan pillars—I passed through it.
Sometimes, forgetting the cloud, I wondered
at their blindness to me,
and supposed they were laid asleep, each in his task.

Perhaps I was already agèd then in my thought,
for I called those workers lucky,
each morning and evening as I bathed alone,
watching the smoky haze in my mirror.

Most fortunate were those concerned with the temple.
Workmen digging a sewer trench had found
the skull of a war horse, slim, tapered,
pierced with intricate holes and grooves,
like an ornamental spearhead—and blinding white
when the clay and small earthlife were brushed away.
A good omen, they said.
Walls went up around it and the people came,
feeling the presence of the goddess more powerful each day.

Then the time came when the cloud parted.
It was in the queen's judgement hall as she greeted some refugees.
At first I thought it was someone else, not me,
that I saw appearing, reflected in the bronze wall.
His hair was like black light from his shining breast,
his eyes had the white gleam of ancient art:
carved ivory, or silver set in gold.

Fear should have made me hide, but I felt none,
when the queen saw me. And then I heard her cry out:
"Can you be truly he?
The one that Venus, kindly giver of life,
bore to a mortal youth now long since withered
by a green river now filled with blood?"

"Queen," I answered, "you only have known and pitied me.
I will exalt your name above all, whatever land may call me."

So out of nothing, unseen wandering, I was made king.
And sleeping beside her now, my dream is only
the city's future: a rain of salt and mortar.
The work, though, the queen and people go on despite my fear,
without my order. My only tasks are my beauty,
which she takes as ever renewed (but it is going),
and this disconsolate and useless knowledge.

Where the river in its ravine
slides toward the sea, dividing
the workers' houses from courts and temples,
the viaduct is almost finished. Crossing there
to bless it, I saw myself on a level
with tops of tall willows risen from the banks.

Below, ants are starting up the trunks,
there are frogs sleeping, a blackbird clinging
sideways on a cattail, tiger lilies in bloom,
moths flying low in underbrush, a dragonfly,
inch-worms descending on threads...

No time to take the path that winds along
the pilings and go down there, where I've often rested.
For many years now, no time. First came
the king's idle work: inspection, blessing.
And now a god who appeared to me shrouded
in youth's beauty and altogether as I once was,
has made me burn to leave this pleasant place.
If I am not dead to fame, shouldn't I flee
before the ocean, walls, and forests all catch fire?

My love will never change. But I can hear the promise
of the kindly winds flowing from this land.

After Kong

It is right that I, the King of King Kong's Island,
should offer thanks and praise,
now that the Americans have taken Kong away.
And even we, on this remote atoll,
have been shown the film in which the great ape dies.

Our wall, work of the ancient and forgotten
fathers, rose and stayed there out of fear.
In the dark midst of the jungle and the brain
it divided us from terror. Now
it stands against nothing.

On one side all the forest's extravagant plants
and noises, and on this side us. It used to be
that the altar beyond the little man-sized door
was found clean the morning after every sacrifice.
Now victims putrefy and buzzards glide for days

and bones pile up. Clearly we should discontinue
the whole wasteful and demeaning custom.
At last we are free. We eat and sleep
incapable of fear. Lethargic trees
moving this way bring down the useless wall.

The Sphinx

Who knows how to exist? I was
not given the power for this task.
To create what I would be in my own image.
To make a life by casting my body into time.

My body, battered by storms
of ancestors, images, stories:
a lump of clay under the incessant rain...
my body is the thing that swallowed me.

And then it was devoured by what it ate.
For food always invades the flesh it feeds,
and the prey itself becomes the predator.
I am...as though a lion had killed a wanderer
and, waking, found itself half a man.
Now welded to its carcass that had never questioned anything
is a hideous weakness, this bag of curiosities,
barbarous itching of desire at all seasons,
huge sex out of all proportion.

One day I woke, looked in a mirror, and was this horror
formed of two beings fused and stripped
of memory: had they once been separate and complete?

If only I could remember falling from some beatitude.
If only some perfect form had once been mine,
and I could cast it before me on the screen of night,
an image of a former self to stab me —
then, at least, like a wounded man, I would fall
in the direction of the pain
and thus move on.

But I am only these fragments yoked in space
and rooted here. On the day of my creating
men saw in me no suffering, only a monster,
and my legend grew. My claws were their scriptures,
my legs cannons, my groin a city of glass;
one side of my mouth utters the ancient chant,
the other, dawn and dusk, drowns it in sirens.

But everything they say of me is a lie.
I was the compassionate one, the seeker.
In fact I never took joy
in the task of posing the riddle.
No, I performed it as a slave,
a machine at the bidding of fate or god.

And I did not know an answer.
Humbly and patiently I sought one,
inquiring of all who came near —
the cruel, the arrogant, the stupid,
and those who trembled without hope, knowing they did not know.

If anyone returned a question to the question,
I was not permitted to accept.
Every time someone answered, I had to watch
in pity and terror as he shrivelled,
untouched by my fatal claw. I did not kill:
he burned in the fate prescribed for ignorance,
which all are guilty of.

And finally, when Oedipus came and told his truth,
I was not, as the legend claims, defeated.

Rather I thought it best to go away
and attempt to die

because of the confidence of his answer.
Because the one who saw was darker than all the blind.
Poor, without hope, yet it was I
who knew the whole: the youth who answered was less
than the faint images—his source, his end.

And I was nailed to this thing that gazed, content,
at its erect moment,
surrounded by toothless incontinence, dry ash.

But I was also a cat, only a cat
without desires or prophecy,
knowing the scent of grass, joy of the muscles' sleep,
my fur, my slitted eyes, absorbing the sun.
I wanted to slink away and rest.
But the people called me vindictive, a power, a mystery.
With art they caught me in this crumbling form
and left me forever
at the door of the desert and the tomb.

Lucretius in the New World

About 1890 a shadow disembarked
with Italian farmers at New York. They bought—
some of them spending their last money—
train tickets to Ohio, and he came with them,
settled where they worked, wandered the railroad tracks
and the banks of Mosquito, Meander, Mahoning.
Although he loved most the fields
between the firebrick works and the river,
fields filled with rabbits, catbirds, flying grasshoppers,
it was the farmland not far from the small mill town
that came more often to his thought.
It was lush, young, and like burnt Italy
when that agèd land hoped:

"No human presence hurries these pure morning fields,
though a road winds among ripe, wet grasses that sparkle
    like a wave.
Blackbirds perch on wooden posts—
from their shoulders red and yellow flame sprouts out
in the night of their feathers. Everything is cool radiance.
Even, on the slope, the cow and her calf grazing near an oak tree.
Light themselves, they drink the leaves' pool of shade in
    the brightness
lavishly spread.
            And they could be the same two that I once saw
in the Italian glen, the murdered calf restored here to his mother
by some grace of chance, a reconvening of atoms
that have wandered far. I remember how the priest, two thousand
    years ago,
slaughtered that calf. Beside the silent, vacant temple
I saw it fall, hot blood gushing from its chest,

the wavering pillars of incense smoke. My thought
saw also, far away, the mother's frantic eyes,
her restlessness, how she passed the plump willow shoots, rich
    grasses,
the streams full to the brim. She plunged into
the shadow-tangled thicket
and filled all its empty places with her wordless crying. But now
in a country without temples, I almost believe the two of them
    are reborn,
are here by this tree, given back to each other.

                                                    And the whole earth
is given back to me—pure brightness filling space,
the glowing sky, sun's splendour, the roaming stars and the moon
given back to one dead. After two thousand years of death
brought back to the world, though an image, a thin shell
of atoms once broadcast into space from the body of Lucretius.
Only a shade, a question, a pervading eye, a pleasure
that mixes, subtler than mind, with all things
but passes through them, unable to touch.
I have become the thought that I once had
when I was a bodily man but in my mind I pierced
the walls of space: all was transparent, a clear sea
that held many earths. I quivered with godlike delight
to see that airless, unpeopled world, and know there is no hell.
There would be an end to the man Lucretius,
the child he was, the fields he loved, his painful
wish not to die, and the poem's long work: to know
and hope in death.

                            And now by an unheralded resurrection
all is given back to me. Even this cow, this calf,
reborn—although to them rebirth is nothing,
their deaths are nothing, because they don't remember.

They don't remember the ancient separation, ancient pain,
they don't know their pleasure here as a redemption.
Even if they are the same as those I saw,
the same atoms, the same bodies, they are new, remembering
    nothing.
In them there is only warm circulation of fluids
through vein, throat, stomach, intestine, udder,
only the sun's strength in the brown fur,
only presence to one another.

                        And presence to me.
Their bodies restored. A blessing beyond all thought.
The earth, and all bodies of the earth,
given back to me, except my own—
given back as pure vision, not mine to touch or move.
Pure brightness filling space, the clear sky
crossed by the roaming stars and moon. All things
given back to one dead, a shade, a questioning eye,
a ghost more deeply within each thing than itself.
I hug them all, the outer forms, the inner workings,
bathing each atom, filling the voids—
unknown, absent, joyful in everything."

Evening

As I sat on a hillside, eyes chained to dusk,
chained in pleasure to the ash-golden going light
on white pine, black willow, silver poplar,
maples all shades of torches, oaks cased in molten bronze,
the ruins of the woods falling, twisting in a breeze,
a billion lives, leaves, flashing,
floating down and ending there where night
already welled up around huge roots and trunks,
the leaf-fall thickening night, night deepening the fall,
the placid evening swallowing the hot autumn noon,
birds silent, bats and insects swift and still,
I wondered again how joy—true joy
yet without exultation—could come and always does
from this lessening of things, of colours, movements,
number and speed and happy confusion of thoughts.
And I saw that I was two, there were two in me:
one returned and triumphed, the other one fell,
and the dark one rising, like a king deposed by his son
but now restored, was mourning the son's fall
while the bitter youth went down to the dark cell
graceful, passing burden, crown, and hope
to this old one, now the new, who takes possession
of night and walks under branches as under roots,
wishes only to bury and sleep away his life,
the brief watch of his presence here: and so he dreams
on the hillside, still hearing the young footsteps
dying in the cellar, until at last he's alone
and wonders, Which am I, the dark one or the light,
and which is vaster, which is the former, which the late
and formless, which is male, female, walker, city,
the sea and the sun, the god and the realm of seeds—

a delirium of concepts, but here in night's dampened sphere
a quiet delirium as before recovery or death,
where one as a girl watches by the bed of the other,
the all-but-dead one on the bed of grass and ashes,
stroking him, calling him
to rise up, or as a husband
prays beside his wife in the calm before birth's torment.

Something Else Must Come

The hours when you were naked by
the still more naked ocean
will die. The sand will still stretch out,
floating more wrappers and more bottle caps,
its warmth will lick the breasts
pressed down in it. High engines
will drone softly, as once to you,
from the blue sky or water,
more softly than bees in a red flower.
And you'll remember how they sweetened
the distance that you lay in,
the pure crystal that praised
your body; you'll remember
the human longing, the thirst, which you infused,
white soft form that drank the day's light
and poured the overflow down
to grateful men. As long as he, your master,
the almost tireless sun, held
and penetrated you hour beyond hour,
who could approach and take his place?
But when his heat grew feeble and
he reeled from the day, then your soothed pulse
would take fright and run fast. For now
someone or something else
must come to you, for good or ill.
And I could tell you to put away that fear,
fear that grows and exults over you
now that you're cold and all seems taken back;
I could say, "Distract yourself, forget,
be calm." But I know the dark of each day
would bring you, with humiliation,

with slavery to anyone who deigned
to serve you an exhausted hour,
ecstasy also, nervous ecstasy
that would crest higher even than the sun,
if it left you more alone. Then find,
find someone from within this very dusk
that's thickening to love you. Morning
won't come again, the earth
rolls you ever deeper in its shade.

April Song of Fear

It rained tonight. Now in the streetlight
the bells of one white hyacinth shine
in the midst of a lawn
from their tower a single evening built.

And a worm has drawn its full length out
into the warm soaking air: a thing
so still, so soft, so easily cut in two,
and cut, unaware of the horror of being so.

But I'm aware. Just as I saw the worm
I was striding swiftly,
proud of my fluid beauty
and my uncut male flower.

And I remembered how someone that I know
(not well, it's true, not closely) fell
from a tree in my native town.
It was just last week, far away from here.

Someone of an age with me.
He was up in the tall apple tree cutting branches
when the storm came over Mosquito, the man-made lake.
The lightning flashed, he fell from the tree,

all of his nerves were parted from his spine,
and he woke up changed,
a thing that sees and speaks but does not move:
just such a thing as I've dreamed that I might be.

He was a carpenter and an electrician.
Now this is how he alternates his days:

one day he plans machines to help paralytics,
the next he spends crying: "Seven days since it happened,"

or, "Nine days. I can't believe..." Neither can I.
But you, who have done this, and have power, take
my pride and give me power not to forget
you, whoever you are,

and repair your world before it comes to me.

Song: Passing a Hospital

O don't let me be sucked in there,
don't let me disappear, like that friend we had.
Try to remember. We talked to him all the time,
then one day we heard he was "doing better"
and suddenly we noticed: he was gone,
he hadn't been with us for a long long time.

I hear that at first he felt a little weak,
the way you feel in July when the smooth moist sun
presses you down in the grass, covers you,
and sucks at your breath. But it wasn't the sun,
it was something in the bone marrow,
and they cut his leg off at the hip.

We only get word of him now, we never meet him.
But I felt as though I saw him the other day
when I saw a weed a gardener pulled from the lawn
and threw on a bright sidewalk. Its leaves were softening
on the hot cement, and traces of dried earth
still were clinging to the long white root.

Song of a Traveller

If only I could be the air that fills my lungs.
It enters all their dark tunnels, their branch-roofed roads,
and comes to every end, fills all ends with itself,
and goes still farther, changed, into a new world, the blood,
flowing in calm strong currents, bringing life.

And not be what I am: a tiny wanderer
along the forking paths and streams of my own body,
with always a new turn to face, a new decision,
one way to take, many others never to know,

with always a growing envy of the air
that gently possesses everything—but not
as my hope does, which drags its horse behind it,
and when sometimes it arrives at a place it loved from far off,
it can't bear to stay there even long enough
to cry or sleep, but trudges onward that same night.

The Rise and Fall of Envy

A child, I never yet had envied the dead
or the river or a stone, not for their pure
movement or immobility, or the way they swim in
the light that fills them. First I envied
the girl I'd never be. I wanted to know
her body as my own, to do with it
the things a boy would do but a girl seemed
to have no thought for: to bathe unclothed
all day in light, in water, and to explore—
with the air's warmth as if it were my own
breath and hand—each ripple where the limbs
flowed together or the flesh opened.
And most of all I envied birds when I saw them
sitting in trees at the day's end, then soaring
up to a bar of cloud turned orange and green
to westward. I could see the faith
in which they hurl themselves, at rest, to vast
spaces—a faith not even boys on earth,
the solid earth, can feel—and I looked down,
the tiny details of the world were wheeling
and glowing as I turned, deep distances
floated under my breast and held me,
and all below was the same glory
as in the mornings when I ran in the wet grass.

Debate with a Child

A child talks at night when there seems to be no one:
I was not all misery. Remember the light
on blades of reed and grass. Remember the sky
pulsing over flights of goldfinches and a rusting boat,
the red brick pumphouse, empty and locked, on the bank,
blazing. Even the people there gave me everything,
a way to live: intensest peace, peace that burns.
Their life was not always angry shouting:
the lightning bugs and streetlamps under maple trees
became my thought. Who else but those people granted
the moist loam-scented night, the street and its silence
drifting past calm housefronts to the creek?

But the listener, not frightened by voices, answers:
God only knows what you would be if not for that.
Now you're blind and hold the hand that curbed you.
They gave you a name. You can still feel in the dark
of that street of yours, your ancient world,
in its sounds of water, frogs, and crickets, how
with no name, no need to make small objects
with your fingers and lips, you expand, grow,
and join this night you always say you love.

All Is Patience

A world is in me, is exactly the world I'm in,
with its unremitting sky—blue, grey, or black—over cities,
its concerts of music, murders of composers,
stasis of antelope, speed of concrete highways.
And still in my world in me
there is no time, no body, and no space.
The weather is despair that follows exultation
that follows despair, and no night, no exultation,
resembles another. Buildings crumble daily
to titanic splendors, the carved gems in a ring
on an infanta's finger: mine. Sleet and sun
fall through the walls as though they don't exist.
And even though everything there is always new
the same dead have been wandering through it,
hammering together its pyramids and forests,
since I was born sitting in a vacant lot.

I spend all my time struggling to let this world
escape from its shrinking shell before I die.
How little I've opened up, how little of it comes out
and that little changed, dulled. In the mirror
I can see myself frantic in the world I'm in,
see stillness of dark eyes, lip sleeping on lip,
time flowing motionless in coils of hair.
And within me all is patience: the sky there
does not crack with dread, trees tangle in wind
but never in panic, a rabbit stops and eats,
a hawk shifts its head, looks down, in crowded cities
people are hungry, others eat, on the prairies
herds, wolves, and thunderstorms are calm.

Savage

On a high level of the pine tree there was still snow
as in a meadow up in green jagged mountains.
The chorus of birds made him laugh with pleasure
though there was no chorus, just many kinds of birds
in late winter trees, their calls sometimes gathering in peaks
to make a rhythm as waves and traffic do.

The birds were music to him and he was happy
to be like a man two hundred years old and yet powerful,
like a sun-carved monument or stark fossil,
its own era dead, still burning into this one.
Alone all of a March afternoon on barren
dark-gold slopes—he didn't pretend to be
one of the living. Only a remnant:
a savage, idle, violent, wandering and looking,
without shame indulging in songs and luxuries,
feeling himself fierce, unconquerable; knowing
he falls silent, weak, when the phalanxed Romans come.

The Romans. Sometimes, glancing up at the high ground
to wait for them, he would dishevel his words
as a woman whose husband is killed in front of her
claws clothing, face, and breasts: low shrieks sounding
the injustice of all that can be said.

But they don't come. He's let alone. Or if hurt sometimes,
it's by chance, the way a thresher or a drill press
takes off a hand, or someone's struck
by a car, cancer, lightning. The bullets
are elsewhere. Inescapable starvation
of others surrounded by nothing but burnt hills.

Minds bent to scorn themselves from earliest childhood.
Screams of the tortured. He's free here in the meanwhile
in an alley between disasters,
with a job sometimes, or no job
but enough money to eat badly,
to walk afternoons in the work-emptied neighbourhoods,
talking and singing inwardly, but silent.

As nature seems to ordain, the bird sounds quieted
to almost nothing at noon: now and again
a hard small noise, flung quickly, swallowed by the air
and remaining, fading in his ear,
in the ear's darkness a pinpoint star
perpetually shrinking farther, never gone—
as if all song had been unborn
into its seed, that inner sound. Vastness
was thundering faintly there, from horizon to dark shore.
In it the regiments of music were undone;
fallen, the great walled cities advancing to compel
harmony, establish endless joy.

And almost nothing was left: only the cry
of a goldfinch
flashing in the blue spruce. And then a sharp
barked whistle, a few more following, chaotic,
tuneless: among magnolia buds, warm
in bright cold air, a sparrow's chirp,
the same that often in the treeless street
on a pitted red brick wall
bursts, and a savage starts, hearing again
the music of things, a survivor of dead times.

The Famous Works

The biography says that though the works were famous
by the time he died, he was isolated and unknown.
But we used to see him around here
and admire him for his childlikeness,
the clinging affection that alternated with rage.
We used to marvel—what should we have done?—
at the cherubic white strengthlessness of his hands,
his bloodshot eyes with a remnant of old clarity.

That face and that body—as if an antique engraving
had come alive. A drunken pot-bellied Silenus
sullen in ruin, about to fall asleep
in the warm weight of his fur, his breast rounded like a girl's.
And the mythological sex: we could imagine that, too,
how it would look in the picture
where the artist has lavished such minute attention upon it,
hanging there dead but in appearance like a youth's,
a fruit never to change or fall until the tree falls.
But we didn't imagine: we often saw him naked
when we wiped saliva from the drunken face
and undressed the fat body, laying it in our bed.

If everything has its use, maybe that was his.
When we were tired he was more tired.
When we were sick he was more sick.
When we were desperate, this muffled desperation we can't feel,
he'd be raving drunk and fall, hit his head, suffer convulsions,
so that we were whirled up in the theatre of agony:
histrionic shouts, sirens and revolving flashes of the ambulance,
the steel table of an emergency room,
stolid officers, forms, assurances, a ransom.

And he seemed to enjoy our wonder at the strange,
moving contradiction: a Horatian art, pure, severe,
full of mournful laughter restrained...
and then the slovenly helpless life surrounded
by grey boards, broken walls, dust, the alleys,
the bars where we always found him,
the nausea and pain of those days and his every morning:
signs of a world that sickened us, but in our house
we could say to each other: It exists.

And when, worn out, he was sleeping in the house,
the bed clothes changed and changed again,
washed of sweat, urine, vomit, blood,
we'd walk to the hilltop to calm ourselves,
to prepare for the dreary hell of his awaking.
Silver water shone below at the street's end
between brick walls, there was a stir of distant labour,
of quiet air lightly shifting, one with his sleeping breath.
Maybe it was tears of fatigue at the day's end
or too earnest gazing at the bright west,
but once the sun flamed before us doubled
and was his eyes. Smouldering, steady,
sleepless but moving toward sleep,
it roared and melted silently into the ocean.

In Puerto Rico

In 1949 Juan Ramón made this list
of synonyms: god, essence, noble consciousness,
you, beauty utter and complete.
The thing so named, he said, lives not in its young
manhood alone, but most powerfully in its dying.
He prayed to it: I am swallowed up
and swim in you, wholly submerged,
but in you I will never drown,
as a child never suffocates in his mother's womb;
because you are the blood inside me
and I am in you as I am in my blood.

Worker of bronze filigree, delicate
hard words, undaunted. Many sights
and dreams, even in 1949, foretold
the human events that would compose a face
for that vague loved one he addressed.
Already he had been blown far from where he grew,
from mornings of Moguer, cafés of Madrid,
a world's rightness, what should be eternal, grown a memory.
And then to light in Puerto Rico, agèd
but stronger, seeing farther through more tangled leaves,
new powers in the quaint garden, the little house,
the lecture room, the green museum.

There Zenobia died lingeringly. Alone,
he was weaker, older now, disappointed,
and he fell silent, next was injured in his body,
no longer could rise or move about,
and so died: there had remained more loss,
more failure to come, than yet had announced itself

in 1949. Too soon,
those thoughts of congress with direst things,
the words beautiful, utter and complete.
You, noble consciousness, summed up in him,
drowned in the dust of his blood.

Song: It Does Not Matter

It does not matter how foolish it is,
you need it to live.
It does not matter how foolish it is,
you need to repeat it.

It does not matter how foolish it is,
begin to live again.
It does not matter,
continue to live.

How foolish it is,
it has always been yours.
It does not matter how foolish it is,
now you need it.

It does not matter!
How foolish it is!
Now you need to repeat it!
Begin to live again!

Minoan Bull Dancer

A naked youth gracefully seizes the goring horns
and vaults over the bull's arched back
as it gracefully charges forward.
The tiny figurine, broken and eroded,
a crumb in the glass case: what was it for?
What does it picture passing in an arena flooded with cries,
in a noon under green mountains, white rock cliffs,
shouts of joy, shouts of the hawkers, sidelong glances,
courtship, boredom, childishness, and the sea crawling below—
so that when a girl fingered it at a stone altar cut in a wall
a thousand festivals, shoddy and magnificent, came back.

Still the beloved object shines
and crumbles yet more, and the gaze holds it
as on an ignorant, unclosing palm,
turning it, turning it, as though to see
what people lived. But that can't be recalled.
This image is what's left. Impenetrable clarity
is not to be given up, knowing never exhausts it.
It stands there still, it vaults
motionless in its dance, if it is a dance,
or its terror, provoking
the endless procession of meanings that pass by
seeking their end.

City in the Mountains

Poetry is little except in love.
A mountain, a city stand before our door:
in one, meadows of yellow flowers
and the cast antlers of a stag;
in the other, glass, flashings, swarms of unmarried girls.
Bright is the morning on the snowy peak,
the sunset that draws its brilliant gashes
along wires, towers, a low mass of sea-dark cloud.

A great thing it is to be seated here,
a petty thing to be fumbling on a sheet of paper
with signs, dull and small. And you could pray
years for a word to blossom from what you see.
But they lie there already as formed, in dust,
hammers in a box, congealing tubes of oils,
and fingers scrabble through them in face of the huge day.

But that city, that mountain. You can go there,
in one you can fall on the bleak granite,
in the other on concrete and the legs go past you
like scissor-blades of a clock, a billion clocks,
a billion copies of one clock in an infinite store.

And poetry is great again. As long
as there seems to be beauty, it knows beauty,
light falls on the snow, light in the highest story,
in blank facades the great longing, as before.

Death of a Sparrow

The twisting dance of the sparrow, delicate
agony, as it tried to bite its wounded shoulder:
circular flurries, brief trembling flights
and fallen landings—then the wait, panting,
a new try for a low perch, a try that fails
and the contortion of brown feathers falls back down
in grey dust and the light green maple flowers
shrivelled, littered there. When I approached,
a fury of terror possessed the sparrow, racking it
with useless struggles, pain, exhaustion,
more terribly distorting the poor wing.
Understanding that nothing could be done
I went, and saw another sparrow fly down,
and the two bob a while as sparrows do
in the high unmown grass and dandelions,
companions. Then the strong one was off,
a willing arrow, gone, curving into the trees.
The next day the sweet body in the grass
lay there, calmer than it had ever been,
even in sleep, in the life of the hungry sparrow:
the winged shape in death more winged still
after pain accomplished slowly, unobserved,
in a long laborious night, once all had flown.

Cicada

Locust outside my house,
sing, deepen the boredom of the afternoon.
Thrust me back into the old vacant hours,
oppress no more with fact that in the empty
expanse of childhood was still unknown.
Prey of the wasp, grinding your wings
there in the leaves, here in the glowing curtains
don't sing of agèd summer, your sexual death,
but of endless brightness, saving shadow: sing,
deepen the boredom of the afternoon.

The Aeolian Harp

Because music is always indecipherable,
the language of God's prophets, as Luther says,
it alone having power to solace human fear,
people once found us wonderful to hear:
instruments of unwilled music, whisperers to the air
in the air's own voice...as if it had a voice,
as if it had an ear. And then for some reason they forgot us,
so that all the rest have been destroyed or lost,
for all I know, and I'm the last—left here,
trapped in this window in the Alps,
never to be finished with moaning.

I can't claim to say anything of myself.
Yet is it possible to speak and be nothing,
to form thoughts and have no will?
When the old king loosens his yoke
under the icy rubble of Mont Blanc
and wind comes foraging through yellow flowers,
then, but gently, I scream harmoniously,
a misery that would tune the wolves and thrushes.
The four strings moan a thin, antique music
without octave, without rational intervals:
a single chord that wavers from sharp to flat,
from silence to confusion:
four notes that never will sound separately
or mix in another order. What can I do?
Some tongue from an earlier creation wakes:
as if a sage had discovered, in the earth,
the polished pelvis of a dead monster,
a groin shaped like omega, honed by eons of gusty sand,

and strung it, following some notion of the Orphic lyre,
so he could hear the dawn-time speak again.

Here forever within the limits prescribed,
these sounds that suggest a dream half hatred,
half shackled kindliness:
all things destroyed and made new, for good or ill.
I summon beings that are earth and man at once,
and claim the strength to drag forms out of space.
Fins, tentacles appear on cats and dogs in the suburbs;
at noon, now winged, they spit out fire along the sidewalks.
Sometimes I make moss spread on women's lips,
or change the bullet in midflight for the assassin's eyeball.
The ancient death song of the swan, when nature
was touched with knowledge and an appeal went up from innocence:
it seems, next to my new music, the meek invention
of slaves, a bow to fate, to the death prophesied.

I summon. But where is the world that lives?
Dream of an old bone without sinew or joint,
strung like Apollo's lute, jammed here between
a vacant room full of white sheets
and the valley where distant flocks move imperceptibly,
huge clouds are chewed by wind above the glacier.
Day after day determining, never starting
the praise of what I love.
At rest I hear myself sigh far away,
my voice not even an echo, my pain not pain,
only the quiet veil that falls at the end of a question.

Puissance Nue

Reading, he came to *puissance nue*,
and who was she, this naked power?
Toward the name hurried all the sweetness
of a confused dreaming desire, of feverish
watchfulness, part dalliance, part demand.

Yet naked power in his English mind
was only bull-like stupidity armoured in brawn
hungrily stripping each sweet thing of its husk.
Impossible it seemed that *puissance* could be power,
power's beautiful cousin, descended from the same root;
impossible, however long the words were read,
to see that strange nakedness, the *nue*.

Then suddenly she appeared, lying by warm clear water,
asleep on thick grass shining under violet leaves.
And as his look prolonged itself she grew
more open and more bare
to eye and light, the stir of liquid and air.
Yet dark was not abolished: under those trees
and in her hair, in her body's furrows
it played, mixing with daylight at the doors.

And also a man slept with her, calmly naked there:
the same one who walks these littered streets in disordered dreams
stripped, proud of strength unwillingly disclosed,
and trembling—because the devouring stares
are just up ahead there, the jeers, threats, blows
of naked power huddled, darkened and stinking,
in its never loosened purple clothes.

Beirut 1982

When I first came to Beirut in 1957,
I was a spy and everyone here was a spy.
The streets were full of maharanis
with green stones between their eyes,
and each green stone hid the plans on microfilm
of another weapon that could destroy the sun.

Everyone knew exactly what everyone was
and what he wanted: the women, the plans.
And so we tried dispensing with cumbersome disguises.
Besides, as they say, the best disguise is no disguise.
Get rid of them all and you might be invisible.
Of course, there may have been many invisible spies
in Beirut in 1957. But most of us clung to the last,
most tragic and alluring incognito.

Those were the days.
Nothing but jet-set princesses naked on the beach
or in the casino. The roulette wheel went round and round,
the chemin de fer went straight ahead, and the women
lost and lost from the inexhaustible funds
of fat opium peddlers at their backs.
Or they were mistresses of arms merchants
and wives of diplomats. What agonies
they suffered dining on hotel balconies:
boredom, regret for innocence,
lush hair, and buttocks sheathed in light.

And how much they needed to be refreshed!
Sometimes the women spies would hire a yacht
and the day would be one long party on the sea.

The decks were swamped with ever shifting
and opening white waves: they lay
on their bellies, waving their toes in the air,
whispering and playing cards. We male spies
were captain and crewmen, waiters and bodyguards.

And the Mediterranean was more than clear,
it was a telescope that magnified
how every muscle in every thigh
beat its tiny wing as those women
with their snorkels and spearguns floated through
old wrecks and drowned Greek porticoes.
Did they succeed this way in subduing us?
We were frantic with longing and, by turns, with pleasure.

That was before the civil war. The dark ages again,
Christian and Moslem: they take things so seriously.
When they shoot someone, he is maimed or dead.
It was different among us spies.
We used to get beaten up, tortured, cracked on the head
a dozen times a night, and go dancing afterwards.
The ones who got killed were only lumber anyway:
beefy torpedoes who never had any childhood,
who never existed at all, until suddenly
they were standing there on guard, always looking the wrong way
as we crept up and dispatched them.
The enemies of freedom would have us in their power
time after time, but never kill us.
Instead they'd dump us in an abandoned barge and wait
till we came back and destroyed them. But the kingpin
would always escape: an aristocratic mind,
servant of a totalitarian power,
tragically conscious that history had bound him
in the end of things, as an agent of the end.

He would always rise again, we would always defeat him.
We would always have victory, he would always have fate.
Those days were eternity, were heaven.

Now the F-16s go whining and pirouetting over
on another bombing run. The old
Nazis and mafiosi have fled from their pink ocean villas.
The jets come in low, I see them hit their targets
or maybe just anything: an anti-aircraft gun, a house,
some women the guerillas are hiding behind,
and the hospital for hydrocephalic children:
there are four hundred of them there, living in their own dirt
now that the staff has fled.

And the spies have all fled to Hong Kong or Rio.
Everyone left here now is an average character:
old women in black robes, fat men in plaid slacks,
shrieking, hugging themselves,
swaying in the streets all day, all night,
sometimes putting a limb in a little sack.

And no orders have been sent to me here for years,
so provisionally I stick to the first assignment:
to find our friend. I'd never seen him,
but they described the man to look for:
even if he has failed, they said,
even if he's surrounded by torturers
and knows we can't acknowledge his existence,
even if he wants to let death come, or kill himself,
or is already a dead man, he'll remember us,
our cause will be enough for him and he'll live.

That day so long ago, when his call was cut off
in a strangled gasp, we didn't know where he was:

maybe Leopoldville, or Vientiane.
For twenty-five years I never knew why they sent me to Beirut.
Now from my room on the Green Line
I can see tank trucks spraying disinfectant
on the rubble heaps that cover rotting bodies,
and children unmoved by the whine of incoming shells
dragging heavy buckets of water home.

To His Subject Matter

So I'm left
to exalt your mere deaths equally
with those that were most greatly mourned,
your lives that would be forgotten
with the vanished ones that the living still most long for,
the ones they still try to follow,
looking on the ground, reading the welts and crushed
pebbles and grass, ruin, as if some ancient passing
footfall had blessed them.

There's nothing in you,
minor versions of great sorrow,
some small confusions
of mighty self-contradiction and bafflement:

the wrecking storm, brilliant and vast, scarred,
healed by lightning and its quick decayings;
it passed through here a life ago
or in our sleep and gave its memory
to the frigid, rain-whipped,

cowering…Leave me alone, you, of no
imaginable good, with my small part and
never-to-be-repeated view of power.

Protracted Episode

Then I saw one who, biting at himself,
dodged at us through the traffic. His plastic neck
stretched so his jaws could reach his shining buttocks:
cunningly made. And as he chewed he said,

"It's no unworthy task to create a speech
that ignores everything this time thinks true:
helpless patterns and correspondences,
the machine of age and endlessness of death.

This speech would be the song of an old man
praising his own eroded voice as though
it were the glory of mountains and the withered
centuries, his bleached bones were their bright snow.

But to project this man, his voice, his song,
is to confess the other speech. He is only will
yearning both to forget what should not be
and cut a swath through it with his sharp brow.

He is a voice that wonders while the flies
circle the bearded grass-tips and the stars
burst on the mountains—wonders all the time,
chanting perplexity and willing praise."

So many tears then filled me as we stood
in a bank's shadow, and so much desire
to guard these words, I quit my guide and journey,
came back, and tried to remember all my days.

June

Late lights in a few houses, streetlamps lost in trees,
a town far out in the fields, alone, shines softly,
a constellation, points of light, dark spaces.
One motion only: uncertainty of leaves
in lightly disturbing air…until time passes through
in the stillest hour, rattling along its rails
as though it assumes this place has need of it.
Then from its window a passenger glances down
and, startled, thinks he sees himself out there
walking in the town after midnight,
wet darkness on his face, his feet sounding in the silence.
Night has destroyed the petty kingdoms of house and lawn,
he crosses vague frontiers of scent,
the lilac's sphere of influence, the hawthorn's.
Each step in the complacent night is a choice,
hard forcing of the will. All motion here must be chosen,
each minute choice is harder. He comes to the creekbank
and sees the silent water, black, so slow
it seems to stop, no longer flowing from beyond,
no longer going by to other lives.
But here a nervousness intrudes,
slight quivering of body, ground, and air.
A late train passes. Imperceptibly
the whole town shudders with its quiet rhythm.
At once he sees himself as a passenger on that train
awake beside a sleeping woman, watching this town
rise weakly out of darkness and reel back.
Fear keeps him sleepless: the harsh irregular
rapid chatter of wheels beating in his chest,
not soothed by the woman's breathing—too slow, too soft,
perfectly even and powerless. Thoughts shift

relentlessly, recall that the rail line passes through
a thousand towns like this one, muffled in wheat.
Or maybe it passes through this one a thousand times.
Maybe this is the place the train will stop
up ahead, some winter day, when weak light wanders
over fields of snow, through the town's ice-shrouded forms,
and all is a wilderness of frozen fountains and stars.

Home Again Home Again

Your parents had reached a long slow time,
as animals do, the great centre of their lives,
when they gleam in their fells as though eternally,
unchanging. Or as a day can seem eternal
if you lie and watch the full clouds, conscious
of your own time: you soon must get up and leave.
So father, mother, the small shabby town,
its patch of earth going on as though forever: you
forgot them there, where they'd been since you started out
and where you could find them again—as anyone
forgets what he has to lean on
so deeply and heavily that it wounds his side
and the pain seems only himself.

Ungrateful? So you accused yourself one day,
waking suddenly. And when you went at last
to look for them where they always are, they'd gone,
or were withered alive, their mouths opening and closing
without sound. The buildings had leaned still farther
toward the dusty weeds and crumbs of old machines
littered everywhere inexplicably. And now
who will explain them? Your grandfather's day
is as absent from your thought as is your own
gestation. And check the records:
what is written down says nothing.
The volumes all avoid the one question you have.
They're like the notebooks you kept in adolescence:
you turn the endless pages and you wonder,
what did I know or feel, how did I live then,
what was this violence and love, this utter newness,

invention that could sing water and light, raging
at the first touch of dying, never mentioning death?

You went back and the bones of your native town
were like that, records from which something had escaped:
a skeletal mill that roofed ghostly technologies
where men once worked, coughed, burnt, bled.
And that way they had permitted the long pageants
of the children. And of the mothers—whose images,
vague, identical, stalk by in the nights,
each one sorrowing and serene, her starved, enamelled,
hard flesh torn, her dress the blue of late dusk,
the heaven behind her a work of flat blinding gold.

The Stump

They were disembowelling the little woods
to build a school, and clearing out the brush
where we and the goldfinches used to play. We hardly
knew what we were losing. And all one endless
turn of the seasons we were compensated
by the huge stump a bulldozer had uprooted
and left on its side in the scraped clearing.
To us it was a city of hanging causeways
and passages underground. We crawled
the maze of tunnels, ramparts of upturned roots,
from early spring that filled the terrifying
pit beside it with yellow water
to winter with its wrought work of ice.

It was more than pleasure: a place to live
beyond the reach of old voices, of routines.
We were deep in a bleak and secret castle, strong,
beyond the childish pliancy of leaves.
And so I came to think
that grace itself is in hidden things
torn up in silence, turned aside
from original places, first desires.
Now I remember you listening to my replies,
looking to where I stood, quite near,
as though for the star that had decreed to you
misfortune, not willing the harm, itself compelled.
You saw that your heart would have to beat in exile
beside the empty pit of its rightful place.

Fruit of Spring

Trees were newly in leaf, but through a blur
of alders and willows, soft green and hinted yellow,
a bone-like oak stood up, reluctant, unpersuaded,
without a bud.

And sorrow, unheralded,
a new pain of loss, a new love, sprang up through me,
to know the bleak branches would soon be taken away,
buried for six months under the green leaf-world.
Buried, those sticks, cold flesh the colourless colour
of metal corroding, twisted among themselves
like ruts over a bare rain-ruined country,
but companions of my winter.

Perhaps it was easy in April,
my mouth plunged deep in the soft nursing air,
to offer thanks and praise for vanished pain;
perhaps it was easy in full possession of that gift,
that mood of calm espousal, warmth
given me out of winter's long barrenness,
to love the giver and want it back again.
But so it was. Out of a backward longing,
love leapt the coming of fruit and fall to winter,
and not to its brilliance, blazoned white and blue,
but poverty of bare twigs and frozen mud.

White City

The force of vegetation relieves the white city ringed with ice.

Green shoots and buds explode in window boxes…a flotilla of
window boxes has broken through,

Down the river of grey light shrouded with iron leaves and
creepers.

And already the people, released from siege, in the midst of
festival,

Begin to finger their sticks, to glance nervously at the
liberator.

In the unlocked city still piled with garbage, where food and
water were growing scarce, a boy watches the advancing flowers
on the quay:

Lank-haired, too white, his nervousness suppressed by drugs, he
smokes, caring nothing about the outcome of any struggle.

Perhaps the suicide of his mother, or an inescapable gravity of
self-love, the shroud of Venus,

Is the black radiance that hides him from young widows now
filling the waterfront,

And spreads darkness, silences the sap in the dusty weeds here,
stills the blood in the air over the harbour, balks the
unfurling of leaves,

Making him bear to be this unregarded image: life that dreams
   forgetting life, setting toward the horizon he watches with
   unfocussed eyes;

Adolescence that wants to die, submissive to death as to a
   woman's fingers, filling with desire,

A frenzy to burst from the swollen body of this waiting.

Where the sea air comes ashore, where he stands,

There floats an ever stronger love of dawn and dusk, of beaches
   in fog,

Of all edges where the visible spectrum fades,

All borders, all zones of penetration, where something is lost and
   something found,

Where the creature changes form, or ceases and another takes its
   place, of a different order in a new world.

All that was hoped in, vanishes,

With a life that was spent forgetting how the wish to die might
   be a wish to live,

Submission to a benevolent sign. As if a boy in sexual despair,
   dismembered,

Pieces lifted and jostled on the swell, a beating mirror, women
   and clouds…it was he

Who invented death, laboriously piecing a beautiful thing from
  fragments of many others.

Then he awoke from dreams, found himself looking seaward at
  evening,

And saw the product of his sleep rising: the new, long-fingered,
  necessary star...

O nostalgia, hope, someone crying softly, silver trees, silver
  stones in the deepening air,

Twilight slows the blood, stirs the veil of the distant worlds,
  withdraws the colours

In this white city menaced and sustained by green.

April Fool's Day, Mount Pleasant Cemetery

Snow lies in long bright fingers, frigid melt-water in pools.
The sun finds green in crushed grass newly uncovered and shining,
it warms the grey tombstones
while the city hums far away and high white buildings
stare down through bare trees. Alone, here,
it is possible to feel the proper sentiments,
love for the poor, contempt for the oppressor.
Then the young voices of two women approaching,
walking among the graves, talking and laughing softly:
rage floods back. The nearness of anyone,
the pleasant disturbing nearness of these girls,
their vowels like the poised mass of breasts
and motion of smooth hips...A moment ago
the ground here was covered with warblers
picking at last year's berries, coming near. They fled
and now they chatter far away. A crow lights in a maple,
the girls, never seen, are moving off behind the tangle
of yew, young spruce, and cedar. And now again no one's here.
It seems that the birds, always searching in their disordered
anxious flocks, would come to be shepherded,
but these people never leave for long. Also the women
under the stones would come—this one "a victim
of the *Lusitania*," that one dead at thirty of God knows what:
if not for the voices that pass and never stop,
they would come out again and say what they were.

City Limits

Freshness of April morning, to whom should I come
but you to teach me how to limit myself
within vast depths of sun on a red brick wall,
and purple climbing from green: first crocuses,
joyous, impassive, between the peeling house-front
and the huge tires of a truck returning from market?

And you, thoughts that like to wander among headstones,
be glad you're shut in a shallow, unmarked grave.
It closes, and is simple earth where I stand
quietly looking, careful not to break
your dream, while light waits at silent doors
and the sky is a wide street, empty and still.

Snow in May

No one today. Too hard, too white, too brilliant
the park lies underneath new snow, cold light.
May, and noon, yet the city is locked up,
even the streets are silent, as if stunned.
A sullen fury seems to seal all doors
because, so late, heat's irresistible march
is halted for a moment, and the business
of spring is buried. But welcome to this freedom
from stir and noise that a strong sun brings out
when, as in a closed attic through a window,
it warms and resurrects the flies, and ends
all thought, all love, all hope in the distraction
of a chaotic swarm. This, too, is spring,
this snow on petals of the first flowering,
light flakes blown from the new leaves, the blue sky,
and sheaths of ice that bloom with light along
the confused branches of the spindle tree.

The All-Night Café

I like to see a boy writing poems
in the window of an all-night café.
His almost empty cup, his pack of cigarettes
are at his elbow in the papers scattered
over the wet table. He gnaws the cap
of a ball-point pen. The crackling pink and green
neon sign, "Café," muses over his shoulder.
He's living an image, of himself and of this city,
trying to be serious, trying to pierce through
the great illusion that his youth wraps around him.
He doesn't know, can't know, and yet he knows,
writing, that his effort too is illusion:
someday, just having had to live a certain time
will strip it away. He'll be sure that now he sees,
until it happens all again: that new knowledge
will be seen as blindness too, and the eyes are only opened
by the power that, remorseless, drags the unknowing one ahead.
At last, death, the lucidity that is
imposed against the full strength of the will
and only that way realized. But no.
No one can say that, growing onward, always
we slough off illusion and are brighter, more supple.
Isn't illusion a stiffness? Falsehood is stiffness,
and age is a stiffening, death is rigor.
And so perhaps this boy, who twists his body
gracefully, unconsciously as he writes
staring, hands straining, is as far almost
from that last illusion as a man can be.
Relentlessly moved ahead, restlessly striving
to desire what is, still wonderfully far from the goal.

For all these reasons, I love to see him writing poems in the window of the all-night café.

Our Unemployment

This, close to our pupil as the punk's shiv
or the torturer's needle, this twinkling grassblade
wet with morning, magnified
by the way our head is lying in the grass
(the soft grass mixes with our beard),

this joyous grassblade bent and then released,
as between a swordsman's testing fingers,
by sporadic wind, this calm grassblade,
unaffected, between the crumbling baroque
splendours of my vocabulary and sheeps' gazes,
wine-stinking breath from these
would-be sleepers restlessly crushing the grass,

this grassblade from earth to air, shadow to light, free,
is our unemployment, idle
pleasure. I think with disgust
of the wife of my years
and the daughter of my youth. Go. Breed
more nothingness. Or don't breed,
be nothingness yourself. No more clinging
to breeding's insults, womb's pain, breasts bitten
in shacks for the sake of infants
such as I am, heavy body caked
with scabs, huge muscles hanging dead
on long bones, helplessly maturing
into the age still to come. In the recesses
of thought, the sun on my neck
and on this grassblade,
my nerves purr, I look, I am content.

The Worm-Picker

At night the worm-picker wanders
in the wet grass of the boulevard.
Bent double, he slowly moves his flashlight
in the little replica of ancient night
the dense maples mould under the street lamps.
At this hour, in this city of three million,
not even a car is barking. He works,
gently tugging at each desperate worm,
not letting it snap in two
and return half to the earth.
He drops each captured whole
into an old coffee can tied to his ankle.
He goes quickly—each minute of the night
is precious, times are hard—in the priceless
quiet: even the window over there, where someone
wrestles all night with a bank book,
glows calmly. He straightens up, this field
exhausted, and for a moment his cigarette
covers the scent of the mock orange in flower.
Then on to his old blue station wagon
and some other scrap of grass ringed by concrete,
where the worms come up to breathe
and picking is easy, as fishing must have been
in the beginning.

The Ruined Cottage

Women and men from whom all had been taken away
he tried to show me, and so took me up the stony mountain
into the first world. Wind inhabited the fog,
there was the howling wraith of his own childhood,
as the sun rose, burning the world clear and laying bare
the naked height, suffering its own love of the dawn
among scraped rocks, a few twisted shrubs, the sparse
but greenest grass, and flocks that blew at random
on the slopes. He pointed to cairns, inscriptions, names
of people who were forgotten, to two foundations—
for a sheepfold never finished and a house
crumbled—and to dreary places along the road
where once a dying, silent, blind old man had trudged
and mouthed and dropped his bread. Then I looked up
and it was all gone. Dawn was stabbing from the west,
a subvitreous dawn in the green mirror facade
across the street, and in this fast-food place,
the vistas of polished floor and ceiling tiles
and orange and lavender Arborite, two scabbed drunks
are arguing. The few other persons scattered through
the acidic light look around or stare into their coffee
or empty Styrofoam: afraid now to walk up the blocked aisle
and ask for another cup. Beneath the incoherent violence
of the men's loud words, the rest all lie like mummified
berries under a tree putting forth spring growth:
something about whether the city knows how to pave its roads,
and whose are some dimes and quarters. One sits, the other
tries to stand over him but staggers, runs sideways
to save his balance, falls against two ragged girls
feeding pancakes to two infants, and lies unmoving
in the spilled syrup, plastic forks, and screams.

Don't you have any respect for women and children,
says an old man, almost in tears, don't you have
any pride, any manhood, are you men? The sprawled man,
insulted, lunges for him, and falls again, cursing,
against the young mothers. And soon it has all
been swept away: the manager has put out
the drunks and their antagonist, and the two girls
have mopped the coffee from their clothes,
quieted the children, cleaned the spilled food from the floor
as if this were their house, and pushed their strollers
into the snow starting to swirl and drive. And I know—
when they first came in I looked up from "The Ruined Cottage"
and saw them pool all their money to buy that food.

Indifference

It
is an indifferent world:
nothing is different, difference is nothing.

And there already you have all the words
needed.

Why then are you struggling to get by heart
the name for each detail of a Greco-Roman facade,

and studying in a medical book the terms
for every suppuration, every tic and scab
of that vagrant sleeping on cement
and spotting it with bloody saliva,

and trying to call up words for all the colours
in a flotsam composition, even the names
for shades of shadow that mounded kelp throws upon
a green blouse and a silver bottle?

I remember cotton mills that now are less than ruins,
that now are hated in indignant, unread books alone
for invisible pain they caused, pain cured at last
by the vanishing of those who felt it. Since 1780,
the dying beggar has wandered with me,
although his want has died in the eternity
of his earthward gaze, the eternal sufficiency
of his chance-gathered meal.

Love in vain. The animal
that suffered dies and pain

flits to a chalice in another field
an age up ahead, deeper into the sun.
Here on the brown dry clay a stone recalls
the starved weavers.

I observed how the memorial, once huge
upon exhausted and deserted ground, dwindled
as glass offices sprang up: this soil
that had seemed dust became the wealthiest.
The doors revolved, their leaves flashing in the mind
while they turned perfectly in the parallel winds of men,
as the leaves of trees flash in the wind of heaven.
The flocks ate their lunches on the illegible memorial,
and all was happiness. Invisible there,
watching, I was abolished from all care
for the names of colours, the floral organs,
the machine parts in the plants
and my own body, that ticked, advancing
to register the power of the sun and meat.

A Postcard from Havana

It arrived today from my Mexican communist friend,
tattered, with a blue picture of a tattered city
in the worst white geometric high-rise style,
and with a message on the back: *Estoy
pasando unos dias maravillosos en esta ciudad.*
Already, perhaps, the RCMP has read it;
in their scarlet tunics the translators by now
will be daydreaming of old silver planes
rattling out from Miami over an indigo
Caribbean, dropping down to the enchanted island
garden of floorshows, gold flowers, and casinos.
All of us have been playing a long time
the game of innocence, of taking sides
with right-minded fighters cutting their swaths
for natural man: meanwhile it's death that walks
one side of us, close walks the other side.
And poets are paid experts in death and ways
to live with it when you are the one left living.
The beauty of certain elegies is this:
they can be read aloud beside a campfire,
the eyes can weep, the hearts grow proud and angry
while the hands are still free to clean rifles.
Yes, but a boy—and not just any boy,
the boy I would have been in El Salvador,
Honduras, the unruly one who didn't enlist
in either regiment, who loved night and violated curfews—
a boy was shot by one side or the other.
He lies dead now in the morning on his stomach,
and someone has twisted his legs outward until
the toes of his feet point to the crown of his head.
I doubt he'd read Whitman or Vallejo, or had time

for accommodation with death, heroic rage,
lovely sad reflections, building against the dark.
I didn't know him but I think that he
was the true partisan, the underground fighter.
He loved his life, the people he knew, the painful
prospects before them, sunlight in their crumbling
village streets and dusty trees, and hopelessly
he hated all killers with an equal hate.

The Ducks

He has seen an old couple seated on a bench
side by side, ignoring one another
but linked, beyond his seeing, beyond the air,
like two ducks drifting on a pond. And then
suddenly in motion the male moves off
in silence, the female comes quickly, silently
behind and then abreast, and when he pauses
she drifts ahead, slowly, waiting along the line
that he will take, until he comes. He once heard,
standing at night on the shore of Couchiching
in the black and fog, a billion or a hundred miles
from wife and son, out in the blank invisible
wetness beyond him, the communion excitation
of the flock. The furious answering and conflicting
squawks. The kind croaks and wingbeats. The harrowing—
with soft necks and edged feathers—of the darkness,
of the heaving frigid slate of waters. But it is
warm to them, a supporting breast neither loved
nor feared nor known. Not known but part of them,
late fall and the coming of dense brutal skies.

Storm Window: The Moth

The giant moth we saw between two windows,
trapped in a locked house, as we were walking,
stopped us a moment: how
it clung to the inner glass

impassively, moving its wings slightly
in torpor. It was like a mask in a case,
with two vast eyes that glowed
violet, rimmed with gold.

But ours was helpless love. So we went on
under the rain of maple seeds in the wind.
The heads of trees were exploding,
the attic windows swarmed

with many fragments of torn sky: shattered
peace and shattered forms driven across it.
Then, fired from ebony,
came random shots of the storm.

We cowered. But we ran with a strange joy.
Exhilaration, sudden death, in the air
and in our breasts were joined,
and the great moth we'd seen:

what had it been, a map that chance had drawn
of our world? It barely vibrated its wings
as if not to feel again
the narrowness of the space

where the wild, perfect pattern had an end.
In those wings, trembling, heavy, the moth bore,
hooded in dust and shadow,
every colour, every form.

The Tulip

You looked into the tulip and came back.
    In there, in a moment, you lived a hundred years,
and how many endless ages have been yours and mine—
    in flowers, paintings, monuments, sympathies.
Hours walking around cities where we don't live
    are like that: towers rising up, pyramids and domes
of many-coloured glass as yet unbroken,
    beyond the low horizon of Edwardian brick:
shops selling tattered magazines, on a bright street.
    Cities not ours, where under the huge clouds
torn by a strange wind, bitter and exhilarating,
    utterly new to us, your body doesn't trouble you.
We've walked in those stone castles carved from mountains
    in a blue vista above the shoulder of a saint,
and always we've gone home: to our own place,
    the one that presses on your shoulders with a weight
we want to call more-than-human, and stoops you,
    cumbers your gait so that the wide-shouldered
swaying pace of young perfect woman can't be yours,
    troubled, in this city you love too well.

Conversation with a Widow

Uncle Johnny died after rigid years
of cutting hair in his shop downtown.
Toward the end he cut it badly, breathing
a whisky scent into the tonic, talc, and
glossy male curls piling up on the tiled floor.
He died shrivelled, a man who seldom spoke,
still with that nickname, Johnny, last
taciturn hint of a youth who may have been
angry, a lover of women, filled and lightened
by vast ocean, the sky over America.
He spent his time at home, silent,
or sometimes in bars, or on the corner
by King's Newsstand with others like himself
on sun-baked cement, spitting single words, standing
in dark slacks, short-sleeved shirts, and suspenders.
The tall and narrow-waisted new world
had by that time completely rejected suspenders.
And after the funeral Mary, his wife, was crying
and said to me, "Why is it that the men
always die sooner? Do they just give up?"
We stood there in the church of our fathers, who
explained their own deaths, all death, by an ancient crime.
How foolish it would have been to tell you, Mary,
something about deoxyribonucleic acid,
adaptation of the sexes, effects of the hormones,
or social factors, things you'd listen to blankly.
Better to say that what we find in ourselves,
whatever weakness, we ourselves have put there.
Both of us knew enough about men's weakness.
Your question didn't need an answer: I
simply shrugged and silently, without real hope,

asked to be absolved from the fault of men:
Powers of earth, give me the male strength
that we desire, kindly strength, which protects.
Don't make my wife a nurse, helplessly
to watch me dying drunk and before her.
And do not punish me for pride because
I've asked to be so strong: to be the last.

An Old Man

Now, still, these athletes in the street
are as young as when I was a child,
are the same who then filled up and seized
all light, all space.
The dark corner left me is the same:
humiliation. Trembling, meek,
closing myself within myself for fear,
I am the small one still,
the child again, forever
awaiting my power, their decay and absence,
the field of my exultation.

And the girls ramping in their eyes:
the same I desired and desire.
Still young, still innocent they are god-born
and fated.
Then and now, one nudity lightly veiled
among the winking signs,
they are displayed to me transfixed, the same
immortal beauty, invincible mirage,
virgin dust that can spring,
made woman by the same
tears at the same betrayal.

And only one thing has aged,
weakened, and already died:
my hope to grow strong and triumph.

Christmas Decorations

The frozen city burns mildly
and the fires barely touch the soft grey cold.
A slight, veiled fire in a window where a woman
might once have been undressing. Small hard fires
fastened in place of birds to naked twigs.

In a cellar under black pines, a mother holds her breath
to suppress a cough: a child is sleeping against her.
A very agèd mother, awake all night wondering:
What will it all be like when I'm not here to see?
Will the ice be more ice, the night more night,
the city farther, our life more misshapen and quiet?
For tenderness, for fear of disturbing anyone,
she keeps her cough, age, wonder to herself.

That child died long ago. An old man
with ice in his hair watches a city bus go by
at 2 a.m. through falling snow, lighted and almost empty
up a long arterial street. How warm it is in the bus,
when you have the fare—the kindly silent driver,
a rhythm and swaying almost like sleep,
dark houses and storefronts pass, a dream,
as though the route and the night go on forever.

So what if you've stood where a door was being closed,
stood in the cold dark, cursing?
Be quiet, pick up and go.
The low clouds, the snow, are the colour of fine ash,
reflecting the blazing city, and the bus is gone.
Know what you have. And bless all travellers.

Prayer

1

Do you feel nothing
but pity when you look at me?

Because so easily, so often,
chance takes away
the few
desperately loved possessions of a man:

movement,
power
to see, hear, touch,
and speech.

And then
still living, human still,
what is he? —

lying in perfect darkness
in himself.

But make me, titan
of a fearful question,
tired of this strength.

Through this fret, within this barrier
of bodily fear
come without pity
and find me.

2

Let my amazement, Lord,
burst through the grief of words.

Not to express
the barred immensity,
light's source, incessant distance,
a promise of repose.

But as a leaf still hangs,
twisted and beaten by surging
freshness, October noon,
only to show
how in that vista
I am shaken.

I Saw You Exult

I saw you exult as the morning grass was drying.

Then came dusty noon with its wooden poles and cables.
Cars passed down straight roads along barbed wire,
along the skeletons of rusted works,
or glinting ribs for new ones being built,
laid out in order on razed plots.

Rust stained the roots hiding in the ground,
the violet flower that ironweed
held high above the dust, even the breakers
of yarrow seething between
a railroad right-of-way
and a chain-fenced millyard.

There you were: naked,
your head a black glory richer
than the snakes of smoke from the steel mills
intertwining in the sky. For the first time
you saw yourself, I watched
the terrified unbelieving
opening of the eyes, and love that struggled
defeated from its birth.

Le Paresseux

Naked—even his sunshade hat and his staff
he's laid aside to lie back on the soft young rocks,
and the pruning hook and scythe have dropped from his hand:
someone else will have to wield them, later.
But now the landscape ripens, dusk
spaces recessional to a glowing distance,
the feathered trees unknown to science,
a long aisle to a just-sunken sun.
In this, the latest light that is still intense,
somehow unburnt by the years of wandering
unclouded noons, he almost sleeps,
wrists hung among stems, fingertips in the grass-tips.

Distraction, the girl in coffee shops,
to her left a cheap clay pot of flowers,
the angry colours bursting in deep sleep,
ravished, against the flat conflicting background
of littered tabletops she's wiping, of chipped
crockery, of moons and melon sections daubed
on curtains buckled, faded, by light and wind.

Here he can see a tree hang down its oranges
toward his unclosing hands, and stone steps,
long worn hollow, rising up the stony hill
to a small temple woven of saplings and thatched.
From it the fruit would be unseen under the leaf-crown.
Could not be reached or tasted with the eyes.
Would grow, sway, fall, unknown to anyone
who climbed and looked out in that frail house up there
for the storm, the night that so far never comes.

The Traveller

Once the sun used to rise every day,
in its light how feeble the man and woman became,
shouts were broken, doors opened
on flowering lilacs and the road.
A traveller who hates his destination, his one hope,
absorbed, walks quickly
with a loved memory he won't recall:
there never will be time. Just once
he falters between the river and his speed,
to dream of a vast thirst bringing insanity before death:
a girl who has as yet no breasts
but knows already how to strip and bathe
a wounded man, his wound that has made him safe,
spread open on the grass, for a child's curious approach.

Dark shining dawn. The creaking of this sufferer's
slow collapse frightens women in the next room:
homeless women, their houses burnt, collected sleeping here.
Their purple eyes, as if cut, as if beaten, open wide.
Crying, a long night slumped against a wall.
"Welcome, son. Though you left us and you are the one
who killed our men, we've made our bodies ready."
Afternoon exhausts itself once more outside this house:
ready to be cut, ready to be planed and nailed,
the nervous trees age, darken, and quiet down.

Morning, Loneliness Died

Morning, loneliness died, dark heights and valley burnt
and you were there, sunlight on your darkened bricks.
From deepest ore the last of metal was disappearing:
engines—how uncertain they were, repetitive, I heard,
they stuttered, fell apart—dragged you without pause.

In white light someone opened a letter far away,
looked, threw it fluttering on the pile. Crowds
jammed through the passages, overfull.
Sweet with unreachable, unendurable sweetness,
a simple music—two notes, one time—
went on and on to crush your watery
returnings of the dead, never to leave you.

Joyous, impassive, you did not permit yourself a comment
on stone, steel, crane, drunkenness, window, star,
a dream of significance. And the hard wall of a woman's
afflicted skin, a man's laboured breathing and scabs,
might torture some, but you don't sanction any outcry. Wind
in a thin tree in the lee of your walls.
And where else is there? Rain. Your loud dead,
lapping, drowning each thought,
whispering under the tires.

Secrecy

The boy was found naked, murdered
in the course of no one knew what shame, and they carried him
    into our house,
his red hand cupped on his genitals. Amazement:
my mother putting aside once her disgust
laid his head back in her arms and washed him gently
for burial. Tenderly washed every part of him.
This happened once. Why every day do you repeat it?

Your fingers were stumbling on the piano, stumbling in the waltz,
agèd footsteps, a presage of drunkenness.
Everyone in our family was old, our younger sister the oldest,
our family come from nowhere with no stories,
no skill, blank faces, only laws.

Stand again in the long gone iron swirling of leaves
under silver maples torn apart, glinting unconquered.
Thrash with your rake.
Heap dark gold mounds of leaves the wind deranges
under that white wall and brutal window,
bare end-of-autumn grass to the longed-for snow.

In the tearing, hissing air around this house,
if a calm hour comes, deep blue, dazzling,
it's rage worn out. The wrecked stone heads,
male and female, persist, always eroding
very slowly, by the bedroom's broken door.

So writing an endless letter of your anger
never set down. So many august feelings:
would a century be enough to give form to even one?

And then the rest would have breathed themselves away
with the slow grey river, the mists, the fireflies
rising among these houses in that just-ended summer.

Fresh Grave

The dead child who passed through here centuries ago
was looking for something ancient,
something close enough to endlessness to be worthy of song.

Maybe a bound sheaf of wheat and a sickle
such as are minted on coins, but standing in a field
and not simple gold or silver: the colour of dying fire,
the colour of bread, of an old tool covered with earth and rain.

She went by herself and she was angry that couples
and small laughing groups dithered by unkept walls,
or in the long path under the high-tension lines,
or along abandoned sidings—anywhere winter had made
a brown, hard, clicking, glinting garden
of dried goldenrod, bricks, twisted wire, and thistles.

How many centuries has she been dead? She walked
a whole life long without ever coming to an end
of our neighbours, our streets and houses, this grey sky.
Set out after her and long before you reach the outskirts,
if there are any outskirts, you'll find her fresh grave,
her carved memorial stone and struggling tree.

Visit Home

Returning, I saw that land still burnt
under the highway's lash—more than ever. And driving on,
I saw it burning now too from the sun.
That August the branches joined the motors
in rattling empty shells together.

Mahoning's land: its flesh was cracking open
and falling away, blowing in yellow grass and disappearing:
the white sky and low river had withdrawn their water.

Winds mocked the dryness with an idle stir,
a flowing hush over brittle leaves and the sand:
water music, and the creek was
a marsh of brown blood drying in a damp bed.

Crowded along a thousand brittle arms with skin
mummified on the bones (arms, dry branches
that clashed in the wind and broke each other), locusts

were singing. That August, over everyone
who entered its cities, the land held
dripping from grey wrists
the fog-like webs of the tent caterpillar.

*

Dying summer was powerful and greedy
around fence posts, in ditches and vacant lots.

Vengeful summer, unbroken:
calm, the destroyer put its hand

to crumbling edges of the streets.
The invisible fire
that rose out of tar,
out of asphalt and brick
and shook the air and sucked blood,
turning leaves to shells
and mummified hands
and living skin to paper—
that was her anger.

*

In that August of granite-coloured haze, Mahoning's land
was like a burning ash about to crumple
while it still holds the shape of the leaf it was.

Dry blue showed faintly through the rock-red air.
The slopes and fields and lots were powder:
a human hand
could sift them,

could search for that land in the ash of its own body.
Where was it: under slag and ore between the ties,
among baking lucky stones
bared by the lake's retreat, below the old waterline?

Burnt, dried out, crumbled,
it would not let me remember how to love it.
Almost asleep, I twisted in the night about to break
in flames, and reached to touch its neck
and it whispered: Not until
my water returns to me.

But it seemed an ocean of sweet water
was dispersed above us, almost ours: at night
it sweat on our dry ribs and cried
in the silent strain of trying to exist once more.

*

It seemed that Mahoning was preferring its own death,
that I saw it struggling to forget the other
that had been brought to it: all the muzzles
of cattle and the human snouts
lined up at its veins: titanic herds
poured out of black steel barns,
fouling the stream below the sea-green hay,
there, where three oaks lean out from the bank.

There water eats at yellow clay and undermines the fisted roots.
In shade the white seeds winding down are a memory
of what nothing remembers: unseen, the wet arched darkness
that once was here, its kindly light
and cool paths. I used to think of it
as the interior of a happy body: rich black labyrinth
as of lungs and a throat beneath a calm, closed mouth.

But could I, by the drying river and land,
prefer ancient, unknown summers:
unknown, or rarely glimpsed by the early people,
who in twos and threes had passed swiftly, hunting
the beaver, their own god? Could I prefer
the forest fire, lost glory of unpeopled August,
to reservoirs feeding the sea of grain?
Prefer that mouth of ashes
where the lightning once destroyed
the fleeing deer's household—

prefer that power to our smoke
that rises even out of snow, our phalanxed
blazing intent on the eternal
behind the blast furnace door?

Kingdom and Leaves

Kingdom and leaves: a child joined
these things together. The kingdom of leaves
runs from the low branches in your hands
up to the sky. And you can go up there,
climbing the branches, and rest inside that world.

The chimneys, balconies, and roofs belong to it
and it belongs to the sparrows. They are the children there.
As if on lawns among gardens, hedges, and houses,
they veer in their ragged crowds through secret shortcuts.
Pleasure is a maze found out in the summer dusk.

And there is always one flying far behind
all the others, who never stop. Kingdom of evening,
coloured like branches collapsing in a fire.
Crimsons pour from ash-blue clouds,
which wait now, and new cool distances,
new, humid lights appear—from how high up
and how far away sleep comes!

Centuries Ago

Worn voices were whispering amounts
in the next room and sometimes would cry out
or a body—perhaps a forehead—would sound sullenly,
muffled, against a wall. Mute noises: Anger? Sobbing?
Impure mixtures, the voices, blows, the rainy wind, empty
flat-bed trucks clanking their chains under the silver maple tree
that night, slow crushing of concrete and black grass.

Summer dawns in your room, child: sunlight and living air
trembled in white curtains and threw them off.
Your body, self-revealed, naked to invisibility,
standing at the window still. And there is the archaic
word of prayer,
Thou Lord, scrawled below in burning dew,
and carved in the bark of a pine—those voices,
hands once, planted it centuries ago
to commemorate your birth.

Founders

Beautiful in its distance
the day burning down and flight of stars,
quiet in your eyes, disaster so far away
it is still forgotten music, ancient peace.

Incomparable, this human world: the vast
plain of black roofs,
light and music at the quiet crossing where five streets join.
Full of joyous prophecy is the flight of heraldic sparrows
in shifting rivers, childish, self-willed
flocks unravelling among elms at dusk. Women decay,
and houses stand open, orange light
streams from the torn eyes and mouths. Others are dark
as though ruined, abandoned last century
or this afternoon: in the distant day of the founders.

Hidden in a moist culvert with booming frogs,
tracks gleam bronze in the low sun and cattails
flow with white molten flax congealing.
Dusky slag. Purple thistle. Empty flowering fields,
guardian lights and chain-link fence. Decades, rust
made lace of black factory hangars on the river flats
and the red west burns through: pattern and quiet glory,
steel decomposing, new fire.

In the park a boy and girl stopped under oaks
and revolved the names: of the city, its streets, this park,
the long dead owners' names, their races
sunk in quiet shadow, fireflies and empty streets,
this black paving or ground.

Shouts of children, dwarfed
in the vast pleasure of coming night.
Arc, fall, thud, splash of balls and swimmers' bodies.
Evening, the eyes, the coolness of young skin
shining near water: such evening was your temple,
temple of pure distance, stones crumbled to their vacant form.
It was you glimmering, you the statue there.
Men in troops passed in through high burning metal doors,
hammers the strength of a thousand could never lift
fell in order, they felt that thumping in the ground
in their frames, a surer heart.

And here you were faintly smiling, not forgotten,
impassive, choked with prayers, worn by hands.
It was you who gave yourself up, your brow painted
with stars and massifs of cloud, your dance and voice
of frog and snake, cricket and locust, your age
more ancient, younger than the naked August night.

Gave yourself up without a cry, with your memories
of a people from far away, strange minds that built this place:
some were stunned at the fading, the mercy,
the strengthlessness of your memories.
The whole injustice of the earth—isn't it here?—
the whole failure of the blessing, in this wooden calm
of faces, walls, obscure
spaces, passion, peace. Too happy
for oracles, a father's or a mother's voice
mixed with grey slime and mist where childhood's stream
bleeds from the ground, you still were blessed with peace
by the one unknown.

Factory Shell

Here, this beaten iron, this steel shed
in the river meadow, this black hangar
empty, where you could sleep—
night is inside though the thistle
flares, purple, in white light
against the wall.

Over there, across the flowering
deserted field and crumbling street
are the houses, wooden, unpainted. The sun
breaks on yellowed peaks,
on a vacant doorframe, a tethered
sheet that streams out and sweetens
on the wind. But here: the corroded metal
houses of this giant town, by the ragged
bank, mosquito-hung, the rusted tracks, in brush
crossed by one faint children's path.
Some are partly fallen:
steel plates and beams
sown in the ground.

Here a high black doorway calls
for a human body, much vaster than your own.
The shadow there:
if your thought had a thousand
bodies you might wake it, settle it,
and make it work again. But now your dwarfed
shape, darkened, your sombre ears recall
eyes, mouths turned
to a hoarse furnace,
the unrecollected breath

of the newcomers: once
they moved darkly here, red faces
blazing, eagerness annealed
in the haze of the pickling mill.

Mosquito Creek

To a stream
light flowing, liquid sound of night,
sparkling to relieve the
heavy, unmoving day, the cloak and kingship
and browning heat of August...

to a dark stream your first
song attached its words. To a stream,
rapid, placid, clear,
a muscle of the earth, source
of pleasure. To a river
as eternal.

Now that song
knows
it shaped itself between stricken
breasts: festered creek, first
love, clogged vein,
thickening wound. There is a green
that veils the ancient threshold, the clear
surface. There is an old carp,
addled wanderer, gaping,
dazed, for breath on the broken
cement of a stair that sinks down
into the grey water.

Now that song is
remembering:
it proclaimed knowledge, once,
of unending freshness,
drawing from this stream its source.

Now it sings to itself:
you are not the one who began from fresh water.
You are not the one who can
declare again
as at first
the clean desire.

Bonham Woods, Bank of the Mosquito

Today was health
and empty sadness, empty
hands, under the bank,
hidden, in airy silences
veined with water sounds
and swallows. The sky
copied its colours, its calm
from the quiet of
the slashing wings. And far
within the moisture
of this borderland, the frogs: voices
as of water itself
belling to mate: unwavering song,
of comfort inconceivable in frigid
darkness, deepest content
in slime
under the pickerelweed.

Is there a way
through day, through evening?
The guide is wild. Just now
it pressed its furred head, small,
eager, against your palm,
you felt its breath.
Sleep-in-waking, it pants,
it butts your hand, runs off,
comes back to where you sit
unstirring, lies down by you.

And everything waits,
breathing slowly here. Night comes

along the silvered road of water
under oaks leaning
from the bank. Night,
motionless, the stars
repeating their steps again. This:
this is the way
to be going down the path.
The hour of bitterness, without air
or coolness, light or shade,
without warmth — don't let it be
the end of this day,
of my memory stretched now beneath
the tangled, untended
branches.

Lost Content

You couples lying
where moon-scythes and day-scythes reaped you,
browning fruit falls and sleeps
in tangled nests, the wild grass,
falls from your apple tree that still grows here:
cry for your dead hero, his weak sword, his flight,
that you were slaughtered and your bed poured whiteness,
the issue of murdered marriage dawns.
The streets crack, a house falls open to the air,
sun and rain lie on the bed.
And the river still runs in a child's hands
under the factory's black hulk,
four stacks that used to bloom with smoke
over shining leaves, beneath thunderheads.
Then the storm
shatters and beats and after
in woods
a scented smoke of light,
a dripping quiet, and the small gold snake
sparkles at the pond's edge.
But who is he? What were
the goods he made, what became of his loved wife,
his children, and where
has he gone, fearsome, powerless? The silver
path of air from the river's bend to its rippling away
beneath the low concrete bridge
is still pure. No one comes, and the child
who watched by it has vanished.
Or sometimes he appears for a day, a night,
in the walls and windows reflected on the water,
in goldfinches' flight, cricket song, the heron's great

rise from the bank. Last a carp leaps,
voices and a lantern slide down the secret stream
in black and gold peace,
past the child's husk, the family never born.

PART III

1998–2000

What We Loved in You

What we loved in you was this, your knowledge,
your closely guarded treasury of sorrow,
miserable self-regard, a helpless poverty
you hugged as the one thing that was yours alone,
forever augmented by inexhaustible futility.

It was a redoubt
against all progress and the planners,
like a walled convent or a menstruation hut:
secret impregnable fortress of superstitious guilts.
No one but you knew what went on in there
and you weren't telling.
Shut up inside, grimly defended, your sex,
your picture of yourself, your love, writhed in secrecy,
cringed in self-doubt, preferring above all things
their own confusions

                    and the hunger
that whirled them into random outbursts
with always, later, tears
of shame that masked an inexorable pride:

pride that for a moment you had bared yourself,
had darted out,
                    magnificent and naked,
                                        dripping light
like heavens in a storm.

And I Should Talk

And I should talk. I too have vied for the title
"Most Disconsolate, Most Wise"—a whole life spent
swaggering masculine splendour across a pitiable text
all error and inelegance, longing for consolation.

Now I think, sometimes, that never again will you
let the glory of your breasts
                              flood over,
never again will I
skim that light
                    like a pelican fishing at sunset,

never leap in it again
like the paired dolphins and their young.

Pure animal gladness
                              was given us without measure
but we darkened it with the second, questionable light,
the lampblack, of always waiting for an end,

always feeling ourselves
        dragged screaming away,
            riving the homely wood
with clutching resisting nails.

So Much You Fear the End of Things

So much you fear the end of things,
and resent each baffling rebuke,
that now you preach the boldest colours, unknown before,
while your own palette grows pastel:
a major composer in a minor key. O the wet beauty
of your random recollections and fortuitous word-choice.
They well serve a meaning that has outmaneuvered
all help till the end of time: that it is very sad
and powerless, the way it is,
whatever it is. That to know it is very brave
of you, very beautiful, furious, and gentle.
Noble, in fact. Nobility has at last come again.
And how sad it is you know well, having stuffed
so many splendid, deeply savoured evenings
into gnomic dearth, your scraggly line
that is an infinite
wave: goodbye.

               The simultaneity
and equal prominence of everything in your style
and here with us tonight
doesn't bother me much, if it doesn't bother you.
Nor do I mind the crepuscular
coolness and shades of violet that temper it all:
the nenuphars and the microwave, our new
complete freedom of utterance and the strange
restrictions—the way we are flummoxed and balked
by everything, just like before.

New Storytellers

New storytellers,
              trying to invent
a new story
        wholly different
from whatever it was
           that came to grief here,
using its jetsam they
               find still floating
near this shore,
        trying to write
a story nothing but questions
        yet adding up
to the end of questions...
        suddenly last night
exploded with their papers.

The gobbets of flesh fall fast,
sullying the mud, and the intangible
ashes of the wreck sift down, choking the summer night:
a warning:

           we should shut up,
indulge our love of ancient reading
and go quietly to a longing grave.
There is an endlessness of passion in contemplating
the glowing gaps and strangely fitting parts
of those ancient badly memorized reports,
but to try to forget the well-beloved,
the sickening old sound and produce another
only brings an end
in mortal nausea.

To us what is given is to listen.

For we have experienced much,
and it was all exactly as has been said:

we have been pilloried,
lain down in ashes, fought wars, and wandered on the sea,
on the great river Ocean and at last
on Lethe, Styx, or some other,
where we now sway in the reeds.

Morning Again

Morning again. Ah, we've gone nowhere in the dark,
we are still here where we were: what a relief.
You get out your guitar
and look down a long aisle through the reeds:

a thousand shopfronts,
brick buildings all one height,
poles and wires dully glinting,
and among them the green leaf-clouds
of a few hopeful trees
memorious of forests—it all extends
out of sight, to the horizon:

                              now, here
you have to compose a song without coming to an end,
although you despise that particular imposture.
But it's the only thing "meaningful
and appropriate to our experience."

Except perhaps to end
without understanding you have ended
but still going on, not believing
or liking what you say.

At least in your music you are never satisfied.
In the depths
struggling, half asleep, to be content, you are
not satisfied. That much, sometimes, almost,
we're sure of.

The General

While I was planning my campaign—very carefully, to be
   invincible, designing the strategy, collecting the overwhelming
   force—the enemy grew so old that it was shameful to hate
   him.

Our propaganda, our irresistible self-justification, fell on the
   whimsy of some old men and many more old women, in that
   country of widows.

Then we swarmed across the border: bayonets flashed through
   human suet, grey meat that sagged earthward and slid from
   the bones of its own accord.

The disease and stink of that country offended our celebrations,
   but we held them nonetheless, having waited for victory so
   long.

Now we possessed the field alone, and I went out into the corn,
   walked and stopped under the gold sky, heard the rattle of my
   sword and restless clashings of dry stalks.

Artisan and Clerk

Like ghosts leaving their bodies those factories
were leaving us. Their black hulks were lying here,
complex and empty—but we heard that they

were in fact still living, elsewhere. Their souls
had flown to a heaven called Brazil and there
had taken new bodies, glorious, in a new world.

The caged and vented fires there, we heard, the power
of the renovated hammering, the titanic outputs,
the inexhaustible eternity of the materials,

and the labour of that world were beyond our imagination,
and the way those mills shone beside plunging rivers
fresher and wider than our oceans here,

the way they stood in the shade of primitive trees and eyes.
And we were shaken by a further rumour: of a flaw
in the world, in being itself, and even deeper—

a flaw in salvation. It was said that those ghosts,
even beatified, were eating heaven—that despite
infinity, they would soon consume it all,

have nothing left, and start on their own bodies.
Was this, then, what awaited us? Not likely. We
were condemned. They sat us down with the manual that said,

"If you are seeking work for fifty hours each week,
then seek for one hundred. Forget sleep. Work
at having no work harder than you ever worked at work:

then you will find work faster and when you find it
you will have learned how to work. Remember,
all who seek will find, and so, think what it means

that you are still seeking. Remember, there's work for all,
but unless you try harder than the others
they will get it and there will be none for you.

Take their work. It will teach them to work better.
You will have what you desire, so think what it means
that you are unemployed and want to die and do not dare."

I remember that when I wrote this manual we were happy.
It was a difficult, long-drawn-out job,
what with the committee, the management, the board,

and even the shareholders demanding to approve each word,
and in total agreement fighting over the drafts,
differences without distinction, hoping to compose

by mindless opposition something perfectly insipid and bold.
Months, years went by, I was paid well
for my work to be erased, and when we could

we huddled together in the depths of the house.
We had and raised our child, we fought and cried,
watched the birds in the garden at the seed

the manual paid for, though they were free in the wild
to take their glory elsewhere
and find what seed they would.

Then it was all over, the warring factions
were satisfied, the self-help manual
for the unemployed was finished and so was I.

And now that, to help me, they put it in my hand,
I have to contemplate the perfection of my work—
no future book can equal its inescapable clarity—

and its uselessness—neither I nor anyone
will ever find work again. Our child, for instance:
when we were employed we trained him at dire expense

with the greatest artists, and he had already created
his famous series of workers, changed into light and money,
circulating through the elongated noplace

of fibre optics. But now he draws graffiti on walls,
dodging the police, for who can afford canvas?
Or he breaks windows, scrapes stones over marble facades,

writes manifestos on stolen fast-food paper napkins,
identifying himself with the subtle, relentless
markings and destructions of the wind and rain:

for no one is going to buy him any other press
and lithographic stone, no bank is going to invite him
to carve the divine history with all

its demonic grotesques on the new cathedral's door.

Science

Knowing that girls once went naked under slender palms
didn't end my desire for these women
in mud-and-sweat-caked nylons.

And understanding that everyone closes the door, the mouth,
and does just what I do in silence —
this only left me more secret in myself.

I learned our open ways contradict the cruel past
yet felt I was rightly condemned,
chained in a black cell, in a castle founded on injustice.

And the discovery I'm like all others, am nothing but others,
is what hardened the darkness close around me
and made me keep alone.

The Source

When the gods begin to create,
their fingers, speed and death,
separate and mix pure masses:
light and air,
minerals and the sea.
Abundance:
why should anything last?
And making and remaking
never
do they ask themselves
will these things come again,
will this day's exact joy
recompose itself,
or is there only so much time:
not enough
for the wheel to return ever
to just this point?

The visibly lengthening track
of a crab too small to be seen
across the rose and gold
wet beach at dusk,
when each pebble throws its own
infinite shadow up the sand,
the sun is so low on the ocean...
of this great work being
lost or destroyed, this evening,
we love most of all
a section of background
in the far left, high up,
hanging in air:

an arch as of purple granite
and beyond it nameless colours,
distilled
in a region where no bodies are
and colour floats alone.

Who cares now
to return to the source,
where the gods' fingers first touch matter?
Better to stay
in this late splendour,
perpetual revolution
of daily wonder, the broken
columns wearing away
to new visages
in the day passing over
and the wind,
random sculptor. Clouds,
ancient monuments — all
are lost, lost again, and found
unchanged. Or remade,
and memory is too weak to know
these discoveries of ours
are old things freshly
come to light, the same
that rain once washed away
and earthquake buried.

Here by the southern ocean
spring
while in our Ontario
October reigns,
wind passing through goldenrod
and tall grass on a hill,

torpid wasps in the pine needles,
dragonflies, the air warm,
with a forecast of cold
that draws in the stream
clear outlines of first red
leaves that float down: things
flowing through a world far away
in wavering forms that are
our bodies
while here now dusk
and the Pacific are our thought.

Egg Noodles

We are on our way to the Generalissimo Nguyen Van Thieu,
the cheapest restaurant in town, she says, but good,
where a family of four (drinking water) can eat
for twelve ninety-five. Despite the name,
it turns out the Thieu is a Chinese restaurant run
by a Japanese family—a fact that can be explained
by various changes of ownership, but I won't try.
We go in and order a couple of piles of entropy.
Preserving the time-honoured fare, the Japanese
have nevertheless introduced certain innovations:
in the soup, for instance, each egg noodle
is equipped with its own miniaturized television.
Goodness gracious we say though gracious isn't the word
but the traditional tea ceremony at dinner's end
makes up for this. More than makes up. Because to prove
that modern technology is not at odds with spirit,
the owners have invested this ritual
with a meditative prolongation and subtlety
unimaginable to the ancient Japanese.
First the tea is brewed, and we contemplate the brewing,
our breathing slows, eighty years pass, our blood
has turned to dust and our bodies withered
like January apples, until they also sift away
while the tea is served, we scatter on its non-existent
currents as the steam drifts up, and swirl motionlessly.
By then there is no one else left in the place
but staff: we can see the cook behind the curtain
in the tiny kitchen making his preparations for next day,
installing televisions in the noodles of tomorrow's soup.

To His Coy Mistress

Your pleasures are immediate,
curled in themselves like any cat,
while the great truck wheels going by
outside our curtains make me cry.
Why am I thus so much dismayed
by transience? Our rent is paid
and I am even at times employed:
we can afford my cult of void
and dreaming it alive with forms—
bodies—as if angelic swarms
of bees, now homeless, yet alive,
blocked out all vision of their hive
burning to less than a memory,
a ruin where the root should be.

Nothing if not intransient,
insisting on what time has meant
by its blank hours, too short and long,
worth song, worth no more than a song,
I have rhymed out the sermon of
desperate sex, the love of love,
to you, the way a priest will rave
at all the absent, while the nave
redoubles his anger on the few
who are there, shifting in a pew
and dozing, warm in their own breath,
content in disregarded faith,
half-watching light-rafts dawn has thrown
through dusty windows cross dark stone.

Rest on the Flight into Egypt

I'm sitting here as if studying the dust
but it's a postcard reproduction in my palm:
Bernard van Orley's *Rest on the Flight into Egypt*,
which is the great painting in that same order
where "'Twas on a Holy Thursday" is the great song.

Earth's perfected beauty, the city that could be,
tall mountains, blue distance, and feminine river
signalling that God will let us stay here a long time,
in this place we loved at first sight, though it is ordained
that someday we'll have to leave: all this
is open in my hand. All this is in the picture
because of the mother and sleeping child,
who need a world to be in. And so there is Joseph,
the grizzled calm old guardian who sees clearly
how helpless he'd be to defend them. So too
the donkey with bright carnelian saddle cloth
and olive-coloured water gourds, feeling itself
loved for its service and nature. Van Orley has shown things
as they are: no hidden interiors
that need a key or principle lost with the Chaldeans
to open, but daylight
on white water, golden cinq-foil, spectral paints.

Life is better now than ever before. Short decades ago
neither this postcard nor any colour reproduction
could have been printed. And to have a small replica
of the dead man's painting makes nonsense of the old days,
when you had to sit alone in the ragged virgin land
with nothing, constructing your own pleasures:
maybe a jerry-built unpainted porch over a valley.

You used to be left either to fail in your own
imagining, or to glory in its power as you made up
some spot of peace between the draining memories
of green Egypt and the frothing Holy Land.
Better not to be alone but have this reproduction,
as you sit in the weedy scrub, moved to blankness
by the grandeur of antique fragments: the breached
beehive kilns and walls of the dead firebrick works.
Better not to be isolated on this hard, used ground
among baked weeds and flying grasshoppers,
black, green, and gold, where the creek flows
past houses without doors and trees veiled
in tent-worm and wild grape and honeysuckle vines.
Better to have with you this copy of van Orley's work
prepared by a huge press that properly
registers every colour, to be faithful, perfectly.

In the doorless doorways the doors are the black
coffin-shapes of darkness within. Life's better now.
Surgery, for instance, is no longer to saw the limb
without anaesthetic. And if some doctor's anaesthetic
conversation spoils it a little, it remains a truer worship
than the praying of lice-ridden crowds that scourged themselves
to halt a plague. New technologies have removed
the need for firebricks, and the steel mills
have been exported to lands where workers still work
long and cheap, lands that enjoy more than we do,
with a more youthful fervour, pouring acids into streams.
Living fossil lands, they show how things used to be
here, when in these ruined shells of mills
workers, like the flesh in crabs, still quivered.

Food's always on the table here, for most,
and isn't that the ancient sign—plenty—that proves

a people and a prophet chosen? The multitude
is fed. In the old days, the crowd
would go out into the desert and behold a story
copied from an older story, of loaves endlessly multiplied,
and not be fed: everyone heard
until he was not satisfied
and at the end nothing was left over.
Yet some, strong or lucky to have a place near the front
with a good view, did come away inspired,
though others fainted or grew bored
at the back of the massed people where they played cards
with the diseased and unemployed
and never saw the speaker or knew what the assembly
was all about, why they had trailed out so far
with all the rest to the pink, howling rocks,
why they trailed back later
to their blazing streets. Each part of that crowd
has its descendants to this day, and they fight
for possession of the electromagnetic waves.

But how far I've come trudging the paradisal roads
of this minuscule copy of *Rest
on the Flight into Egypt*—far,
and all in the wrong direction,
toward a personal and unmeaning bitterness.
In me is the radiance of sun on a clay jug,
a leather saddle strap, the ladybug climbing my wrist,
while the understanding mocks every contentment,
every human thought. Yet all things here
are marvels: a little farther on
is a knoll where the white sun's setting disk overflows
through feathery olive trees, arresting
vision, since they do not grow in this land.

Nothing Happened Here

Nothing happened here—nothing ever
happened in our city, and yet it was destroyed.
What could the innocent citizens have done?
Heirs to two hundred years of despising whoever wished them
    well,
it had become part of their blood: they could not know
that they were proud and dark and suicidal,
that they had grown content to let their own
houses—with these building paper fronts and grey windows,
wedding receptions on the gravel driveways
and burnt lawns—sink back into
a dusk and trash and landscape god.

                              Unshaven,
halfway along to work with his rusted black lunch pail,
passing the dusty trees-of-heaven, blinded
by morning sun on concrete walls of the underpass,
on the road to Gate No. 9, the 16-inch rolling mill,
he told me once: "No human wisdom can build a city
and confer a way to live. Or if it does,
if it was the dead who passed down these flaming tracks,
this schedule of peace and steel that evolves more slowly
than the sun bloodies its hands upward and the species undress,
then it's only because time uses humans the way a flood
sweeps everything down and along,
making it rot, and later spreads some of it on the seeds."

So going around the city while it still struggled
like a beetle half smashed, I saw
some places that answered to the Louvre,
palaces but built by a feeble, violent desire.

Four white marble urns atop the flat facade
of the long-abandoned discount furniture store.
A stone balustrade before a vista of graceful trees
riven by reflecting water clear to the setting sun,
and in a room behind, redoubled
on a closed piano lid, a painting by Asher Durand
of this same view, though he had never seen it.

And everywhere, strange mutations in the slow
but visible decline. The animals we knew in childhood
were all gone now, and nothing survived
larger than a china figurine on a lamp table:
pigeons and mourning doves with asbestos beaks,
sparrows of creosote that slung their chirps like stones.
At dawn and dusk staggering squads of boys
hunted incompetently for rabid, thieving skunks and squirrels,
beat up young husbands, slashed mothers, took
what they wanted, what was there.

                                        The river
is quiet now. Ducks have returned. Remember
how we once saw it, in the steady roar and rhythmic
pounding of the mills, changed to a silver pudding
by some powerful process by now long bankrupt and gone?
It looked like melting aluminum, or the grey slurry
that falls from a milkshake machine on humid nights
when the button is punched. What did they ever do here
but buy what was put before them at the prices marked?
The great seven-story central tower, all cream-white tile,
of the closed dairy factory stands there, set
into the wooded cliff, and two Gothic dwarves
above its boarded entrance
still bear up the beautiful wall on their crushed backs.

That Day

I won't be able to tell you about that day
because though the sun rose, I'd forgotten the word sun,
and birds sang but I'd forgotten those two words,

which I know now and remember having known before.
But that day when I woke I didn't know it was "waking"
or what had been "asleep." I walked in the garden,

the gently twisted path to every vista—tangled
remnants of forest, smooth shining water in a low valley,
the terrace of naked statues: divine wind-scarred

adolescent flesh...I walked in the garden as if
in a camp of cardboard huts on the tenth day of rain,
and in the dark green shade on the blue shore

by yellow iris blossoms (I had forgotten those words
and it flashed across imagination, in place of memory,
that our cold maids call them "boxes of the dawn")...

I walked in the garden: and my soft breath was the cough
of someone dying, lungs filled with salt and blood
that never again can reach the penetrating air.

The leaves on spring-dark boughs were far away
as winter. I sat and held a crystal cube
and turned it in my lap, and worldless,

in a cold wind and a space that were not even
wind or space, I scrabbled at my crystal
with twiglike fingers and could not get in.

What I had was nothing, as the poor say, "We have nothing."
But there was only a gape there, like no mouth
groping to talk, to taste. No nothing. No more.

Untreated Condition

My feet were floating away from me. Already
they were so far I could no longer feel them.
But I despised them, and didn't trouble about it.

My wife screamed and screamed at me as the feet
drifted beyond her. She tried to wake me, shouting,
Why don't you bring them back?

The doctor wanted to tie them down. He wanted
to save them by cutting pieces off: by doling them,
bite by bite, to the ground, he thought he could delay

their disappearance. And he was right, no doubt.
But I didn't want it. Nor did I want too great a haste
in my falling apart, no spectacular decay:

nothing so opulent. Just something small, even
petty: to be, unknown to myself, each day
a little faster, without wanting it, dying out.

Kissinger at the Funeral of Nixon

His flag-shrouded coffin let down from the sky
by a powerful machine. The flag-shroud,
red and white, blood and blank: the rivers
made straight under the beauty of a night sky
revised from profusion to fifty stars
in ordered commerce. Thump of cannon,
concussive wing-beat of invisible doves
over his cradle, in Yorba Linda's air
that is not air so much as brilliance, pure freshness,
and peace, an ecstasy yet a conservation: stillness that knows
to disturb nothing unless there is dire need.

Now's my time to put on muffled memories
of ancient eloquence—"All in all,
I shall not see his like again"—as a suit
that fits badly, just like the common man's,
yet is made of cloth so expensive it strikes awe.
For he was one who climbed to the stars
but never forgot his home. It would be foolish here
to raise again the old squabble over the corpses
of heroes: do they act with will and power
or only as helpless ciphers of what happens?
Did the rage for peace burning in our streets
drive him out of the war?
Was it our valedictory, his and mine, expressive
of our true love, when we poured fire on Cambodia
and released through cracks in the burnt ground
a demon of pure hatred for all things human?
Forbidden by our people to fight another people,
at least we killed until the last moment possible
and so punished both enemies. No question:

praise him as one who never gave up: this much
is undeniable, and admired by all.

And yet our enemies too never gave up.
Standing here out of power I can see them well:
how his indomitable virtue has been made
into a pattern, a method all can buy,
sold on television: tapes
that will imprint it on brains as they go driving
back and forth on the Santa Monica all day.
A perfect machine: whatever stupidity or crime
humans commit, now they know how to proclaim it
blandly, fiercely, never wavering,
to the very end of their lives
and beyond. They pass it down to others:
each vice and triviality becomes a tradition
maintained by the most pious conservatism,
and gives back to its adherents the gift
of being insolent and invulnerable.
Richard, powerful king: I seem to see him
crucified on his own strength, crucified forever
as charlatans tell that his example taught them,
though only primitively, how to bond error
with self-righteousness and mechanical technique.

Better to remember what is fact: his promise
the war would end, and when he was driven from power
it was over. I must clear my mind and speak
the thoughts I have laid out: just now some other mind
was whispering in me. It's as if I had been the mate
of a great captain, but then I saw that we two
were only fragments of someone else's thought.
For a moment I glimpsed an idea we belong to.
And we were jostled by all its other fragments.

Suddenly the pair of us no longer were lone hunters
of the whale-fish. Now we heard the deep intentions
of the whale-people, saw their couplings, the love
of male and female, parent and child; we felt
the divine mercy and indifference of ocean
surrounding and filling them. Also the shores
were with us, because that mind was thinking
at once of our ship and us and the far away
white wooden ports between forest and sea, the waving
women, God's word in the chapel, Jonah, Ishmael,
the outcast on the salt or naphtha deserts
sinking into sand or walking the waves. Was thinking
equally of people from every land, golden and red
and black, and so their power also crossed my mind
and seemed to lie in my bed with arms around me,
in chanted poems and prayers, in spears,
intricate carvings and tattoos.

And then I kicked hard and suddenly was fleeing
through the country's dark interior
on a huge black horse named Credulity.
With one stride he bounded from Washington and New York
to a vile slum on the mountain above Wheeling
and the Ohio. Next like a tornado he knocked down
a town of huts and trailers in Oklahoma.
At his third step he was caught and penned in barbed wire
with other scabbed mustangs on a dusty weedless lot
outside Cheyenne. At every place, squat people
were shouting, "Wield us," and they waved their flag:
the same one he is wrapped in. The fourth step
I took myself. I came to Yorba Linda
to watch the helicopter bring his coffin,
to praise him as the all-comprehending one,
who alone knew the secret meanings of "wealth" and "peace,"

who bore in his own body all we had done
and all we hoped for, and to let my visions cease.

On Distinction

We won't pretend we're not hungry for distinction
but what can ever distinguish us enough?
This country, this language won't last long, the race
will die, later the cockroach, earth itself,

and last this beer bottle: silicon fused by man,
almost indestructible, like a soul:
it will go spinning ever farther from the nearest thing
until space, continually deepening, drowns in itself.

Yet we keep a hungry eye on old schoolmates
and everyone born in the year of our own birth,
and spend the nights in ranting over them,
their money, fashionable companions, pliant critics.

To live just a little longer than they do:
that would be triumph. Hence exercise and diets,
and the squabble over who will write the history
of this paradise of demons casting each other out.

Industry

Thirty years he sat on the dark ground,
his back against the wall that sheltered the harsh table.
An infantile spear of grass towered up between his spread legs,
its open face before his face, one-featured, overshadowing:
bland smile as of a knife edge, green in dripping renewal,
one more among the endless spears in their ranks
repeated out of sight, beyond fallen mills and mounds of slag
to the meadow's forest wall, and past the smoke hills.
Perfume rose from its groin in the mud,
a dark ring where the stem leapt from the root:
it seemed to him the storm's source, and humiliation
when lightning rolled along a glistening brick wall,
and concrete's dust was laid and polished, flashing.
Then the hoarse shouts at the table were drowned as water
was renewed in him, rising, pouring down, covering his sides,
the elm's curved gracious fork, and the pure iron chimney.

Early Machines

The mysterious crane of her left arm
                                    pivoting,
the block and tackle rippling
                          its supple housing,
and in her eye as in a snake's or rabbit's
the obvious, hungry calculation.
                              And beneath:
the useless mouldings of her breasts, the forms
and the fillips:
                like decorations made
                          by an innocent artisan
who once was here
          and prayed
                    and remembered Pan
                              in smoke blown from the smelters.

At night on the watery road,
a white deserted trail glimmering beside the stream,
he would stop the starved weaver, the demobbed soldier,
as they hobbled mumbling.

There are still signs of him: he placed
acanthus on boiler doors,
              grapes and great stone heads on the cornices of banks,
                    he asked the beggar for his story
and took him to lodge at least one night at a cottage
              that shone above unscrolled water
                    sparkling in its sleep.

Secure now in the river's and the beggar's
sheltered peace,

                    he wandered again
back into the deceiving, divulging night,
considering that he knew good
                    of the not-human.

And she: random and exquisite,
the thin beauty tacked across those pumps, her breasts,
for a while blinded me to everything.
For a while it was pleasure
                    though I don't forget
why the stars this evening
          appeared to leap from the sea
                    over the horizon of her belly
breathing on the sand (hers
                    is the shape
that water longs for
in all its shapes and its caressing,
                    its howling
changes). Though I still stumble
in the poor fallen night
                    until the sun
appears, because the earth rolls forward,
and this scrap where we are lying plunges down
beneath the constant fire. I
          like all
                seeing the dawn
                    can't help
                        but say,
"It rises."

                    And winter too
will seem brilliant, when it comes,
          because she loves it:
                    with the artisan's love of rest,

which winter commands: the locked season, of pure
colours and forms burning and secluded
in candid outline, of the forced need to live
sheltered, close to the fire,
on the hoarded produce of dead summer
and once-triumphant arms.

I saw her
loving winter and hope
more than sunrise, because her will
is a machine of that sort which works
on whatever is left—even if it longs
and cries out with antiquated gears
to stop, it goes on working because
the parts were thrown together
to work
until the end.

But the light of this explanation
went out. And in the dark again there was
nothing
but what the eye sees:
the endless, the starving, the prolific,
ignorance hived in winter,
her at the heart of the gaze
and the needful power to love her.

Wren House

There is a wren house invisible now because, as people say,
it's destroyed long ago and vanished: wooden on a wooden pole,
head-high to a grown man as if the homemade house, with wrens
going and coming in their roughly sawn round doors or stopping
to rest on a grainy threshold, is another human face
to look him in the eye and talk. But it's much taller to
a child: up past my farthest reaches the excited wrens
rush all day between their house, the peach tree, and bright vines
sheltering my grandmother's rough red wall—rough dusky red
because it's made with paving brick, not light smooth building brick,
my grandmother invisible too, being as people call it dead.

Both houses hers, one for the wrens rent-free to rhyme their song
of fresh syllables: "Find its central moment and the day
is yours." Now's February, as it was the time she died
and as she died I had to stay—I thought—here in this city,
and be too busy to think of her, preserving my pathetic
job, licking up my substance by writing a lying report
to get some government money for a businessman. But I
do not, for this, see Toronto as a pit like those where now
the Roman slaves dig salt, no light or hope, and no one troubles
himself about their rescue, saying they all died and ended
ages ago and can't be helped or charged now against me.

Wrong, say the wrens, and wrench me back to life. Once I stood
on the asphalt height of the parking lot behind the Church
of the Transfiguration, reciting her favourite prayer to the moon
over the banks and CN Tower, to return her to her garden,
remembering what she told me from her bed after the stroke
at the foot of the cellar stairs: I prayed to all the saints in heaven
and no one heard me. Me neither. What I asked for didn't happen.

But what I wanted? A wren is a mighty being, but to sing
my wants is maybe beyond even him. Whatever can
be destroyed is going to be destroyed. Patience, patience.
Hate what needs to be hated. All is finished. All's completed.

Essay on Destination

I fell asleep, she said, in the bus against his shoulder,
this stranger, and I could feel my head loll and then my body
accept itself and sink down into him. I seemed very young
and very light and small, hardly five feet high,
even if I should stand in my black ankle boots with stacked heels—
a fairy's child, going who knows where. To be so small
seemed right then—it's horrible at this age, nothing
so old should be so meagre except maybe a sparrow.
I knew my body and its confidence had roused him,
and then in the bewilderment of my red-brown hair
the one thin braid, intricate as a cowboy's leather lanyard,
had subdued and chastened his sex again. But I could
revive it. Hardly waking, I turned over (were we naked?) into his lap
and covered him the way an infant half asleep
sucks at the nipple. The spasm when it came was a memory
or vision of walking on a mountain, seeing below the terraced fields
like empty cartons side by side or roofless houses,
red-flowered trees stormed by hummingbirds, and the sun's gold
reflected blue on a beach of black sand. Where were the people?
When did it end? And much later I would have a baby,
the two events unconnected except by the wind of the wings
of pleasure. Where? And would he be with me?
I thought we would always be together on that bus
riding deeper into our country, past shells of blast furnaces,
fields of timothy, corn, and beans, fields ploughed up or fallow,
past cafeterias where Brobdingnagian citizens all day
eat mesas of egg and potato, past the city entirely of silver banks
and on into night, gentle bumps of the road
making the sleepers' arms fall like gates across the aisle,
no one awake but me in the back and in the front
the never-finished never-weary driver.

Power

When the power, she said, went out: those were the days.
Everyone's always calling for the primitive and original to return.
It's very simple: any disaster that's more than personal will bring it
    back.
The private catastrophes dissolve too gently. I remember when they
    told me
they'd shot my husband in the alley. I remember when my son
    disappeared
and only gradually, by dusting the light that falls through the house
in different shapes, different places, every hour,
did I learn he was gone, he wasn't corning back. And I'm still not
    finished,
I still see him in the metal and hear him in the wood crying
as if they beat, they cut him. But when the generators were
    destroyed,
how heavy the water was in buckets, stone after stone of water
on grooved shoulders dragged to always open doors—
shattered and gone. How mean the dust was, how the rain
existed to make it mud. It was what streets, shoulders, water
are for. Power lay quietly clenched in everything
except when it was more quietly being spent
on the struggle no strength could finish with. Is it different now,
or simply covered up? But covered or uncovered is great difference,
only ask a body. Anyhow, if they truly want to have power
back again, they know how to get it, they know what to take away.

Sympathy for the Gods

The women had no sympathy for Athena. She always defeated Ares
    in single combat
but always complained: once she had been the great god but when
    Zeus arrived
was reduced to a bauble of his brain. They would see her by the
    roads in her burnished armour,
breasts overbrimming the plate, flesh brighter and harder than
    the dawn-coloured bronze
yet softer than any mortal skin or breath, infinitely deep drawn
    softness.
Or she went naked, maybe to let their men see her and grow still
    more unsatisfied,
still more irresolute. Might a hero find her that way, unveiled in the
    open day,
and take her? She would bear a child then as a young girl bears a
    dream,
slim as a sun-ray from alpha to omega, her breach a flower, the child
    ineffable.
The women walked muffled up in black from crown to toe to hide
    the human
feminine, its frightfulness or seduction they scarcely knew, and on
    their way to the fields
they crossed over slopes the volcano had ravaged: deadlike,
    mummified in stony scars,
but these lands might bear again in far future summers. Could it be
    that these steep fields had been kneaded
under the burning lava, that they were waiting, were grieving now,
    but they would enjoy
the olive shade, sun-pierced moist-sparkling, someday, for the green
    will return? Whenever the women

saw Athena, naked, lightly climbing that ruined ground, they would bow their heads and spit.

Freedom

It's a green country filled with other-worldly woods,
with distant blue gravity-defying mountains
pierced by great natural bridges and jutting out
impossibly over flower-banked streams. The many towers,
witch-capped, crenellated, partly toppled, all
withhold their ladies, singing but inaudible here
where knights pass up and down the dusty road,
metal anomalies, shining at noon like the pit
of earth or hell might if opened up to light.
One returns covered with wounds, covered with cattails,
dented and corroded, glinting. One sets out
blinding, baffling vision with rays, sapphire, topaz,
like a water drop in the sun. The road of salvation
is a tedious enslavement, the mendicant friar thinks
almost asleep watching them from a fat mossy border,
chewing his oaten straw. An endless round,
the ritual training, initiation, the adventure,
rumours of the deaths of others (never you) who failed,
and then a moment of music and vague light in a ruined chapel,
when what you remember, if you had true courage, courage
to tell truth, is the sting of old cuts and flies,
the stink of rags not changed for weeks. This friar
possesses the vast height of sky, a breeze in just the tops
of the highest oaks behind him, and dark sharp leaves
of a lily next to his eyes with one green pilgrim,
six-leggèd, journeying across. This friar too was a warrior
and rode for Jerusalem once, but maybe he forgets.

Conflicting Desire

The birds are quieting down and in the birdbath fresh rain water
    shines
empty, perfectly calm, as the birds will later be. Evening. They still
    stir now
but don't fly out to drink it, they keep hidden: it's too late for them,
they can wait for tomorrow or have to wait. But he remains anxious
    to touch
the unmoved water's changing of colours into silence…to answer
    its cloud-crossed
semblance of a glance. And yet, he thinks, to live just one day as a
    bird.
To get up speaking unguarded a premonition of sun, hunt all day
    long,
flying across valleys and over rivers, to flurry and battle in thickets,
shine in feathers, and continue, continue sometimes over the body
    of another,
a broken bird, and then go back, stir, and fall asleep as the sky
    whitens.

Snapshot

At the top of the hill you said, "Let's stop the car and look across
   our land."
Patchwork of fields in spring blossom, fields it doesn't pay to plant,
   with rivery green
boundaries and islands: remnants of old forests, sinews of uncut
   willow and sycamore
along the many streams. No end in sight. To north the four black
   pillared smokestacks
of a power plant in meadows along a river. To east the small city we
   were leaving.
And here and there, unpainted barns in hollows, not very near the
   huge white new ones
and their metal silos. "When I was little," you said, "I never dreamed
   those wooden shapes
would lean and fall, the supply of them was finite, no one would
   build them again,
and someday none might be left." Like the boarded-up shops in the
   city
that seems so beautiful from here, if still and harmonized is what
   beauty means.
What is empty is lovely in the distance. We wanted to say this land is
   loved,
or hated. You took out your camera, put it away: no centre of focus
to make a composition. We started the engine and drove down.

The House

It must be I climbed a rise so gentle
the effort could not be felt, and am looking down.
Or it must be there was a sort of door
whose threshold was the ground wherever I stepped,
whose jamb was the air, whose knob was my walking along,
and I've left a rented room and gone into my own house
I never knew I had. Because everything
fills me with pride. I sit and look
at how it shines in the sun, so clean
the carpet and walls, so pure and simple
each item, subtle all their arrangements.
And I pace at night and admire how the glowing
through my curtains from the street outside
more than rescues each room from the silence of blackness,
calls out a muted and so much greater beauty,
stillness that bathes the hot tired feet of chairs
and tables in dark liquid. I pick up and move
a beetle, straighten a stalk, and put them
back again. They were perfect already. Only
one dissatisfaction: over this night,
this single night, every bud of my almond tree
will open, once and for all. Maybe
this isn't my house. Maybe I don't live here.

Immediacy

Cricket chirr, sounded quiet
that nobody can interpret or remember,
say this to the makers of noise: I ring where
the night colours are gathered, far under
the ringing in the ear.

Eternal

Slowly it all comes back, though she doesn't come back.
Again there's the image of ourselves as one alone,
the image we call "romantic," of one
pondering her absence, smoking in the dark
at a bare table with just a cup and a book
of matches on it, or leaning at the sill of a streaked window:
image of one surrounded unaware
or half aware by decadence of city and night,
a beetle struggling on its back in the bed of tall flowers,
black oily shine, sirens, smell of garbage rotting
and of sewers at street corners. Somewhere: a brick
loosening from a wall. Time is stopped
and only she who has passed away seems to be passing away:
everything else, decadence, pain, knowledge
she is everything and is gone is eternal.

The Sign

She has come to the neighbourhood in the arrogance of nakedness.
　　She has come
on a billboard, the one unlittered and the highest spot in among
　　long three-story
railroad houses covered with peeling siding paper of faded brown or
　　green,
near terminal warehouses and scrub lots around shattered brick
　　foundations:
torn sockets without limbs. Behind the bathroom windows she turns
　　her back on them,
turns toward the Interstate to sell tanning butter, like one of those
　　pretty girls
who went away after high school and then is sighted again later, in a
　　magazine.
On her belly in the faraway sand, her legs opened, her openings
　　closed
by only a slight white lace, propped on her elbows so her arms will
　　hide
not all of her breast, she faces out with perfect sullenness, lips offered
and lightly sealed, eyes shut in ecstasy, ignoring. The women look
　　up.
Might there exist such invulnerability as that? Her bareness, after
　　all,
her unsheltered helplessness is only the exaggeration of their own.
Might there exist a smile self-unveiled, a way of walking through the
　　streets
and of lying in the house like her glistening, so that when the dreary
　　sun
leapt down in August it would have to serve, the way the light
　　disperses

over her body and becomes her shining, her colour—an accident,
    as philosophers used to say,
and she is substance. Look at her. Even if her enemies climbed the
    grey painted wood
up to the sign and covered her thighs with sperm stains and her
    greyhound ribs
with knife rents, she wouldn't care. Even if they tore her into a
    million pieces
and she blew away in the wind, nothing would have happened,
    nothing to her beauty.

Uninvited Reader

She notes in the poem she's reading where the disembodied
voice speaking encounters "an ugly old woman"
just momentarily, in part of a single line, in one
of the many long corridors and sharp turnings of the poem,
so that she's quickly lost to view. That's me, she thinks,
I'm an ugly old woman, I who sit here reading this poem
and its ugly old woman phrase and the poet, when he stumbled
over her splayed, swollen legs, registered her presence,
her inheritance, her baggage of limitations—ugly, old,
woman—but never knew, couldn't, because who could
know, who can stop and know her...And this reader keeps
thinking, loving, understanding, trapped in her eye
following the voice on and on while somewhere back in the poem
in a blank passage an ugly old woman sits against a wall.

Maybe

They want to erase you, little married couple of words, but it's not
    so easy
to form a perfect, direct style, without vacillations: ancient alleys and
    stream beds
always pit and scribble the quadrant of the streets. Maybe tomorrow
the general strike will be called. The buses might not run,
men and women finally grow sick of one another,
squirrels and pigeons refuse to stand aside on the paths and walks.
Maybe someone will translate into words hard and definite
as that pure roofline on that November azure the vague suggestion
    of the man
who went outside ten years ago and has never come back in
and still is sitting propped against the sunny cold wall,
his flowing beard and hair patriarchal white but for the amber
    nicotine stains.
But probably not. You, vacant adverb, aside from a full stomach are
    what we have.

Orpheus

He glanced around to check if the treacherous gods
had really given him the reward promised for his accomplished song
and there she was, Eurydice restored, perfectly naked and fleshed
in her rhyming body again, the upper and lower smiles and eyes,
the line of mouth-sternum-navel-cleft, the chime of breasts and hips
and of the two knees, the feet, the toes, and that expression
of an unimaginable intelligence that yoked all these with a skill
she herself had forgotten the learning of: there she was, with him
     once more
just for an instant as she vanished. And then he heard her from
     behind
the invisible veil, absence: a shrill and batlike but lexical indictment.
Why had he violated the divine command, why, when he had seized
all song to himself and robbed her of power to open her own
     oblivion?
It grew in volume and now seemed to spew from an insane old
     mother with one breast
hanging like a huge withered testicle from a rent in her weathered
     gown,
who was being watched by a tall woman, copper-helmet-coiffed,
     richly suited in salmon colour,
a mythical allusion, since salmon were long extinct in the bays and
     rivers here:
songs never brought them anymore. The young restrained breasts
     and the old free one
oppressed him equally and he went to live among men, waiting
     for the crazy
and the competent to join forces and come for him with their
     scissors.
Orpheus listened patiently to my poem and when it quieted he said
     to me:

That wasn't it at all. I sang outward from my face to blue spaces
    between clouds,
to fern fronds, and men and women sipped my song as you drink
    from a stream going by.
What I sang is lost in time, you don't know what it was, all you have
    is your own
old stories about me. And if women tore me into pieces, maybe that
    only signifies
each one keeps part of my body, which is melody among visible
    things.

PART IV

2004–2008

Simile

As if you'd erased the city where the house
where I was born was standing. As if I
had gone away a minute, just to see what lies beyond,

as if anything does, and you swept away my path
with your broom and rubbed it out
with your wheels, crisscrossing it into chaos.

As if I found my way back anyway and you tore
the house down in front of me, but I still saw
you hiding there behind a brick and a weed,

so you tore yourself into dust. As if
over the empty spaces you installed
a loudspeaker with a voice of uniform

and blank-eyed pages, blaring that I
was never born anywhere, least here. As if
the planet vanished then, under the noise,

and I would have to find another one to live on
if I wanted to live. As if in the whole
universe, though, there were now no more,

so my own gorge would have to be that planet.

Memory of a Friend

Through these same rusting girders these same stars
have risen, turned, returned ten thousand times
since I first followed you into this vast pit

of piled materials and shrouded engines,
walled off and locked, as dark was thickening.
Somewhere near here is where I fell behind,

or looked away, a moment only, lost you,
and you went on oblivious, or saw
and quickly slipped between unfinished walls

or past an earthmover's pile of yellow mud,
waiting till I quit calling and went back.
Maybe that's how it happened. Now years later

I'm here again. This city seems unchanged:
only the sense that I'm about to meet you
around some corner's gone. But the night watchman

still is guarding the never-finished tower
against our shadows. Down beside the piers
the sirens howl the same old injuries

and they still echo through our footsteps sounding
in empty alleys: steps that long ago
drowned, listening. The floodlights still reflect

in oily water where our reflections stood.
The sailor and the Mexican immigrant boy
are still being murdered in the barn-like dance hall

on the long street of blackened brick we found.
Between industrial valley and disused canal,
that world still waits, offering itself up

to be uncovered, hinting that it exists:
just as it whispered years ago when a wind
penetrated the dreary college, in January

and childhood's end, first bringing us the foghorns
and odours of the breweries and stockyards.
And you must still be here. Although there are

dead ends, blind alleys, where the circulation
stalls for a time, confused, these streets don't stop
and don't change what they hold. They still lead through

the huddling houses, through black mills, to water
and wasteland fervent in dream-masks of snow,
down to the elements, home and homeless too.

North American Song

I have a mild case of everything.

I starve a little but not like they do in Ethiopia.
Life is empty for me but not like it is in Stockholm.

I'm lyrical and obsessive though not as much so
as a bird: one might better compare me to the bands,
the poet bands of New York and California:
everything repeated, everything lost, every day.

If there's one thing I know, or one thing I know better
than anything else, it's that the difference between mild
and wild is just the inversion of a letter.
By this means the revolution is accomplished.

I'm a little bit homeless and a wanderer
but not like the people sleeping in the doorway,
and am gently rich—yet not for me
are ornate palaces endlessly deep:
no, just a front door, a room or two, and out the back.

I am in opposition but would never want
to seem invisibly strange, so let it be said
that I worship intensity, but not as the living or the dead.

The Helmet

The greatest twentieth-century work of art is not a poem or
  a painting

but the steel helmet: so said some Nazi curator. And indeed the
  German helmet

from World War II that I own does satisfy our obsession with
  elegant design.

Its lines and volumes, simple yet intricate, and the way light
  passes over it

as if it were a planet while the skull-hole is filled with
  darkness: these

fulfill design's one great promise or perception, that a thought,
  even a life,

can express itself with beautiful inexplicitness, and there truly is
  paradise:

the heaven of dynamic patterns and self-cancelled phrases where
  all are equal.

Here is the example, unique for each who confronts it, of a mass
  produced,

ineffable and unsayable impression. Democracy, art for all. Who
  has not seen

these helmets? Millions owned them. Tens of thousands took
   them from the dead.

This one, for instance, I have from a relative, who received it from
   a friend,

a Berber, one of the Free French, assigned with the Americans,
   who taught him

the tools and techniques of modern war. But this man also loved
   traditional means.

At night he used to take a serrated bayonet and pass through the
   lines. In the darkness

nothing could be seen, so he felt for helmets: rough ones meant
   the American army,

and he went farther. Smooth ones: he was among Germans and
   started cutting throats.

This additional work he did for the pleasure of danger and skill,
   hatred of the enemy,

and love of his foreign friends. A stoical man, with outbursts of
   frantic exalted delight,

he went home after the war to a strict life in the desert south of
   Marrakesh.

Now I've turned his helmet over on its back like a small-boy-
   tortured turtle,

and I use it to plant flowers in: those shade-lovers I always call
"patience"

when I know impatiens is their name.

Five Hundred Cities

I'm waiting to hear that my first love has died.
No special anniversary rings the bell:
since many years like frozen orchards ago

she passed beyond my hands, I've felt this dread
always. I wait in fear and wish her well.
What do I wish her: that she live a thousand years,

adding exponents to my envy of her life expectancy,
which poisons the well of modern culture. I wish her
a great poet, truly great yet popular

while I'm a hack in a mildewed cellar
with asbestos dust sifting from the baseboards.
I wish her pullulating with children, and slim as

the new moon, and unbeknownst to me
already dead so that for her it's over, the agony,
oblivion's entrance test: I'm still not ready.

I wish her once more letting me wash and perfume
her starry anus. The anus is on you,
I used to say, and we'd laugh until spring came;

she couldn't get pregnant that way, we'd play
we were two boys and afterwards, I recall,
how serious she'd get: though sometimes she longed to be

a communist and sometimes a nun, she was truly
serious. Maybe she's finally overcome
those terrible swings of feeling and reached the calm

she needed to begin, and now is building the bomb
that will change everything. Naked,
she's building it in some public square because

she's no terrorist, no coward, she disdains
to sneak up on you. All one can do
is watch helplessly, hoping she blows herself

to Judgement and I read about it in the papers
and weep for the loss of losses I dreaded so.
Or maybe I'll never hear, for it happened long ago

but was too unimportant to print. She was
a sober girl who wanted to submit
like fire to its fuel, and by now she must have had

500 lovers, and seen 500 lands, and then
married to make sure that when she died
idiots would be moved to comment, "She lived life

to the fullest and had nothing to regret."
She was the hungriest of us empty shells,
soft and warm and glowing as though the mollusc

had just been sucked out, and that is why
my maleness moved toward her and dead or alive
still moves today, ejecting clots of remorse.

Night of the First Cricket

You are singing alone before the crowd, before
the many comes, first poet, your primitive
and repetitious epic. Canto follows canto
with scarcely a pause, each brief, identical, and simple
as simplest song: "Enjoy your desire." Enjoy, you too,
being lost as you are for this moment in this silence
of your dead of a season ago, and your yet unborn.
The armies of your kind have not awakened, no belovèd
exists yet to hear the music of your legs and come
to mate you with her body, so that soon when you die
eggs of your loneness will wait a further summer.

Simplicity

Once the simplicity of my songs was their meaninglessness
satisfied with what they found, a shred of greenery
that shrouded our house and a larger shred that shrouded
the khaki creek, dark placid with unease, sparkling
of leaf death and offal, a mirror clearer than fresh days,
deeper than a cloudless night its never breaking and
never speaking surface. What else then were my yips
but acceptable amid sparrow chatter and the invisibles chiming,
crickets and cicadas, and the stir, the snaps, the blunders
of big grasshoppers, poplar-leaf-netherside in hue:
sounds of their legs releasing a stalk, that wags now, wild
grass or wheat, and then their claws catching another,
or the flight of one who fell, click, after which we'd find him
impassive, on a stone let's say or bald patch of baked field,
staring wisely, as if the journey had gone just as long planned.
So it's possible to know too much: now, for instance, that dying
was the place I woke to as life. So my first, simplest
songs, a child's shouts, nothing but life, soaked,
buried and smothered in life, lost in life's thorax,
were wrong. So my tongue was moulded by an already old
community of disease and the glories of my eyes were a late
remnant, lute remnant, the feminine lusciousness
and green ray were a greyed-over rind of what had been
before I was formed, a phlegm spit up of the true,
the dead splendour that no one now alive could ever grasp:
our splendour was its corpse
and I had to go forward into the almost birdless treeless
town we had built by cannibalizing the hardened blocks of
      aftermath,
there to fight to live, even live well, as some did,
and fight to take away their words, steal them, deform,

make them my own, stones made adequate
to crumble and tower the song of gratitude that is still enjoined.

Translator

My patched oxblood shoes had the necessary languages.
The left knew Latin and the right knew Greek.
They'd begun with Japanese, learned in the war
against Japan, which was the source of all their love,
root and image of their chosen service: to let my soft
and ignorant feet stride charmed through an exploding world.
The soles and heels whispered in Hebrew and Sanskrit
and toward the end I recognized the Quiche of Popul Vuh
in nails that poked up inside and cut my arches.
Fifty voices of North America that have died,
Carpathian and Celtic words erased—the old laces
held the extirpated tongues in desperate place.

In those shoes I used to plunge along my city
on knowing echoes. All became English as I,
Neapolitan and Magyar, had. Those hard
vessels liked to paraphrase one of their books:
"We hear them speak about God, each of us in his own
language." And sometimes I'd try to learn for myself,
but Alpha was as far as I ever got: first character,
the sign that's the frame of a little house
scarcely begun, or a great house reduced to its form:
intelligible but I could never live in it.

So we'd go walking and they'd sing to me,
maybe the *Alcestis*. Something ringing with hymns
of goats that are gods, with drunken danger and error
and hospitality human and divine, graces
that are girls abashed by their own bodies
grown into loneliness of finished beauty,
and strength to die when the unworthy one may ask—

as surely he will ask. A song of transformation
beyond the end of the song, and beyond all
its repetitions. Have I mentioned these were the last
shoes ever manufactured in the United States?
Often we'd pass a clean stone wall with vines
strangling an inscription, "Out of Many, One,"
and they'd mutter, "Noble sentiment," and take me home
to read "the fountain leaps and flowers" to the mirror.

At last these shoes had grown too worn to answer,
so I bought myself some new Nikes from Japan
and dropped the old leather in the nearest trash.
Thought nothing of it till the strange new feeling,
the strange new shape and weight that chafed and strained,
lightened and cushioned my feet, brought back to mind
something they used to say: "You forget to love
things. That is the true relation: not between
you and persons or nations, but your heart
veined with the inner thought of bird and stone,
broken radio, discarded glove." What ancient author
or modern author in occult, dying tongue
had told them that, and what could it have meant
originally, in its own words, as those old shoes
knew it and tried to carry it over to me?

But then how down at heel and scuffed and holed,
suffering the strokes and heart attacks of shoes,
they'd been at the finish, as their knowledge grew,
and in the rise, breaking, and fall of the smallest verse
they could trace a wave that had passed through seven seas
since earth's beginning. Just before the end,
I recall, they carried me once to joke in pure
American, as we ordered lunch, with a young waitress,
about erotic walks they'd never take again.

And when the girl would smile indulgently
but with true happiness at an urge still strong
in such decay and simplicity, then male and female
were one: and so perfectly at last they translated
the happy despair of some dead epigram they loved.

Love Song

Scorn of flesh spread everywhere, coarse gravy
badly mopped, on lips of the confessed
adepts of the body, checking their hair,
one with the humid dust, in breath-smeared
windows and mirrors. Maybe a sign you were on your way
was there already: over the sidewalk a paper cup
in the fitful wind rolled, wavered, and reversed,
miraculously spared by the dispirited
hooves of the herd stampeding to exult, moved,
stung by flies. Innumerable head,
it trampled through, weltering in hung fat,
a reeling wash of breakers in a hot
glittering. And the flood covered
a poorly dressed woman laughing quietly
with two small sons. Confusion swept up
the banal brilliance of a veiled sky, flowers
hanging bright from balconies, new goddesses
body-armoured, ignorant a wisp of tulle
once among clouds was enough, clinging
between the thighs. And when a sparrow came down
in the crowd's midst and ran across a table
to seize a crumb from under idle
malevolent hands, my thought,
abandoning that street
a moment then for warrens
even more obscure, for nests unseen
and closed stained rooms, darted
with you again
threatened and uncaught.

The Visitors

1

How high, black, in a glowing dusk those two towers
faded over ancient steeples
and jagged rooflines in flat ranks
rising, one after another, to a blocked
horizon. Surmounting the beauty
of lights in clogged cement
forms and spaces, echoing, empty, shining to die away
into shadow, where snow floated under streetlamps,
they stood above our London at the end
of every vista, every wrong turn: the cylinders
of the stock exchange—our landmark, which we circled
tethered by vision as we wandered lost
and at home in the city half deserted
for Christmas, new to us: unseen,
approving everything, like spirits we passed through
the absent citizens, tracing their ways
condensed in that labyrinth.

2

But you, love, never wanted to be free
for very long, alone, private in abandoned splendours.
You wanted the people to flood back
around you, around the feet of those towers
seen above all and looking down
on streets, roofs, humans

passing through their shadows. The full
streets are what you loved
and hated: nothing
has ever yet loomed over them and remained
woman or man. And at dawn the silence we wandered in
was split. Cars rose up out of the ground
and shook us as they passed across
flaming toward the river, and from each
a starry face looked out, grappling or lounging
at its wheel, confident or anxious, driven
to a destiny. Like them, you would leave
no trace, none at all—out of failure, smallness,
and being light,
so that those who come long afterwards can never
find out what your end was. Let them look
back on the wild disappointed
tangle of these streets—geometric fire—not knowing
any one of us who were lost here,
if we were lost. The best thing on this earth
is to be, you said, as if we had not been,
never cry out, leave only cleanness behind.

3

(No struggle's more obscure than this of the windy
shadeless streets that lead, under two black towers,
to an ancient rotunda after many hashed-together
branchings and sublimations. The plastic bags
in the rain here, the plank laid over
a pit of gelid churned-up mud: do you want
someone to sweep it all away, so that everything
we lived and tried will fall into the blank

incomprehension of happy men and women, a future
we once pretended to see blooming from a chaotic
cleansing: from doubt and our wrecking scorn
of every reason, love, and fire? Is that the end
of what you wanted to say?—and is it welcome
in your heart today even if it does not come
till a thousand years after your death? I'm waiting
to see and ask you one more time. But your notes
are not silent on your desk here: the factory hands
and commercial travellers pinioned in brittle
directories, names living now
on the names of streets; and the fierce saint
whose Latin rages more mellifluously
in the storm of your words that pierce his, demanding
to face his God and live.)

4

Cry imperfection, cry
the hammers breaking it down,
the hammers we swung
with a light and cruel
accuracy, ours alone,
feminine and suffering.
Beneath that attack the heroic
relief in crumbs fell
from the cathedral wall: Victory,
naked and complete,
at her feet the lion,
weaving her wreath on the bald
bust of a dead, much mourned, forgotten,
incompetent commander.

In unswept darknesses
of the drafty fane,
in roped-off side chapels
waiting for funds
to be restored,
under rusty scaffolding,
beside the paint-splattered tarpaulin
and the plasterer's caked, abandoned tub,
cry all strict, grievous
imperfection glorying
in our sad fate. Hammer
the mask that stone has been made,
and the marble body.
You in perfect opposition
are only flesh that runs away,
the swift fleeting of graceful legs,
a glitter, light on your
hair and eyes. Everything else
sank down in the clay
of the muddy neighbourhoods,
in a high-pitched sob or droning,
in childish shrieks, and the bass
of a voice that barked its sullen,
anguished commands from a drunken
half sleep. The dull struggle oozed
through the grid of streets,
tarred and cracking, oozed
from closed front doors
and patios, under the weedy
ailanthus trees, their trunks
thrust up in the gaps among
driveways and hedges. Cry:
where amid the shoddy
torment you found there,

the great dull images
already perfect in their grasp
of all that ground... But I saw
your light flash there alone,
determining, and if you did not know,
still it burned more bitterly
brilliant because held above,
held very near above the crying
and the mud. The fire sprang
on its food, the warped
colourless boards, the fissured concrete,
and raged and flickered there,
biting, twisting at all
it was tethered to,
sometimes tearing free
and disappearing, then
returning again from hunger
to exist.

Song

I live with a woman just as wild as I am
with understanding and misunderstanding
if anything can help these holes in the wall.
Whenever I come to a corner of despair
I find her there
before me or arriving shortly after.

And what our love's like, maybe you can gather:
exhaustion, the ceaseless outpouring of substance
to hold back or humanize the wind
at all the chinks that gape in hosiery, house, and skin.
O no one there to knit our dwelling up,
receive us home with soup on the stove
and rose mouth to cherish the blood of our wounds.

This woman's so wild that if as I climb the stair
I wonder why
and yet don't dare descend because the stairwell
descends I think to hell,
she makes our bed right there.
And the ledges of the steps cut into her back
as our pleasures burn and break
the walls a little wider to the air.

Singer and Prisoner

1

As if charmed, you travelled through many tortured
countries almost unharmed, by your god
protected, or perhaps denied
the bounty of suffering. Now you clench your pen
or you call out, and your words cannot give up
music or love while what you want for them
is to be different: to become the new
voice of a man who will never again be heard.
The one who is captured, jailed, as good as dead:
no one knows he's alive. And without hope,
he is the one who has tried hope and found it
not wanting if he still sings alone
the praise of his finished life:
and maybe right now the torturer is deciding
to turn it to a last hour
of inconceivable pain.

If the heart of that prisoner only were your heart...
But you mocked yourself for pretending to a knowledge
that has for its sole sign a scream
unheard. And you refused
even to call his scream a mystery.
That would be to betray him and take comfort:
you mocked yourself for dreaming in his cry
a meaning beneath depthless suffering.
Nothing other sings,
you said, out of that thin dust
of noise dispersed.

What being caught and caged is: who confessed
such knowledge in the rich place where we were?
I remember when I said my thanks and praise
it was not thanks or praise but an automatic
whisper, a prayer dictated by the fearful longing never to know:
O powers of the earth, if I exalt you,
keep away from me. But we already held
what it is to be alone. I heard
your piano and your carefully placed words
incise silence into the worlds.
The machinery of our streets was a vicious
and carefree landscape beyond
your walls, a fretful nothing where the light plays
on shoppers and on leaves yellowing, torn at
by snatching winds: the air, too
violent, wet and cold, ramps alone
among children, admired and feared.
It's autumn: and the windows flashing
freedom, the vigour of joyful lungs and the colours
of fervent elegant death: it was all a fiery
abandonment beyond the closed cell
that is yours, where your questions
examine you, with sharp instruments
probing flesh and brain. And the playing stops,
the overtones go back into air, into dusk:
they were only ravelled ends you'd grasped
of a fabric that isn't yours
to weave—already woven
and torn on a greater less-than-human loom.
It takes back its threads
and knits them up again.

So then in your heart
you made the unheard prisoner rehearse
the well-beloved songs of his adolescence,
of the mating customs of his people. You heard him
at the bars and stones of his invisible cell
singing of low-backed gowns, scents of powder and sweat,
satin cradling breasts that tonight will cradle
hands and heads and liquor in tall glasses. And the flashing
of male and female limbs, the countertwistings
of strong waists as the guitar
answers the trombone bells
tossed up in unison, legendary weapons:
they were answering the bandoneón
of vanished Arolas, and it some grief
of Bécquer, Shakespeare, Catullus: so back
and back. You don't know if he sings, or if
he lives, but his silence is to you this song:
song of a woman (you might have been this woman)
who kissed him and her promise took his breath
to save it, treasured up in her against
whatever comes. And now there's nothing near him
but wet stones and she, if she still exists,
believes he's dead.

3

But you, tenacious love,
will know what is hidden from all. You see,
where no one else but the torturer can see,
that he endures, pain still can't make him
give up memory. Yet in the end
no human strength can resist. Day after day

blankness and agony erode the traces,
erase even the woman. Until there's nothing.
Not even a gesture. Only a loved word,
a feminine name cried out again and again,
impregnated with tenderness.

A scream, a name:
yours. You, all that is left
of the dance, loved hands, loved hair,
words from a red mouth
deeper, more piercing,
more anciently recalled and loved
than the scents of soil and air: a revelation,
a human earth once possessed and now forgotten,
that did not save. If it all falls,
it loses shape and colour, shrinks
to a shriek, silenced, and is thrown out
in the alley with his contorted rind,
you still say: Here is that abolished world.

To the Moon

. . . né cangia stile, / O mia diletta luna. . . .
—Leopardi

Maybe in your extremity, bright moon,
you look down on humans, even me, with longing.
Certainly, watching you, I feel friendship
and always find you full and calm, governing
a clear sky, when terrifying journeys
take me away from my love. Or if not full
then curved like her eyelash or her lip,
a thin frail parabola, the skiff
of a bewildered god hurled and dandled
on a quiet night, the mere of darkness.
Or if not new then half unmade, confused,
ungainly, pregnant or withering, just as we are,
ignored above grey slush churned with waste and
splutter of old neon.

Even on nights of solid cloud or nights
empty except for stars, I felt your benevolence
stood opposite and impassive, watching me
with the look of someone who also lives this life
and knows. As well as anyone I knew
your love is meaningless and would see myself
(by imagination, a power you don't share)
dying with broken back and limbs alone
in a desert or an arctic night, you staring
with your dumb fellowship. And memory warned me too
my era legislates against such symbolic,
violent images, fragments of a myth of pain,
maybe of justice. Ears are closed

except to the daily now,
the real: no one should speak to a rocky
satellite where people have walked and thrown away
their garbage, making the same use of it
as they do of earth. No apostrophe to rock.
My sense and time admonished me instead
to recall a vase where one summer every day
a lover might really have put a single flower;
or the gestures of a friend—critic and scholar—
who died in Venice; or the trip through America
of some proud yet humble hero, a Dvořák or a Mahler;
or some other subtlety, maybe the words between
a great man and a waiter in a dead café
with, in the background, the carnival shape of a hat
once fashionable, the saffron of a blouse
and a redolence of death, as if time passing,
as if being, had almost been glimpsed, going away.

And yet not only did I come back to the archaic,
bare images in me—the moon, words to no one,
extreme deaths—but I saw them in the cracks
of daily things as you stood above, shining
white at noon: saw them even in crevices
between the latest elegant words espousing
lateness, with its consolement, comfortless
knowing. Uncontrollable,
like an antic or demonic force from the dark
of the shrubbery in broad daylight, the brutal
simplicities would spring up. Once on the radio
I heard how witnesses of an air crash saw
the passengers, just as the plane struck earth,
screaming and beating on the windows. They wanted
to be understood, they wanted to get out—
to what? So an endless desert and a wanderer

dying alone beneath you, silent moon,
always came back to me in today's and the city's
disregarded openings, unswept corners,
centres, and ends: the small
cubicles, for instance, hidden behind
moonlit hospital walls.

                                And it wasn't wrong
to deny pastels of indirection, death
alluded to as a sharpness in the flavour of the air,
the idea that the dead one is only present
in feelings of the living one: as if
this is to be endured. Better to let the mind
sink itself in the friend's dying and be dead.
Nothing exceeds your finish, moon, and the culture
of your monotone, colours reduced and harmonized,
finest lines flowing into inconceivable masses:
and yet you are always stark—and most of all
when you vanish altogether and everything's black.

And if it's useless now to say your name,
I keep to this path because belovèd masters
followed it, talking to you, feeling you within
as they felt the shock of their own steps and the stress
of repeating them and wondering while they walked
what you were doing up in the immense
pure sky of April. We still have the prayers to you
they wrote, but what they meant, those centuries...
a cry to one alive and caring? a manner
of speaking? knowledge these two things are one?

Let's say, peaceful moon, you don't express anything.
Still on your face imagination comes to rest,
the dream that you are more than rock

and a reflection, now and then, of natural light:
a sign and so like us
even when brightest you darken and hide
whatever's deepest in you, and endure this failure,
this being an inexpressive, slowly eroded
face of forces you strictly contain—impulses like children
in love with twilight, its plain song and free glide of birds,
but confined now to their bedroom, to their window
because night's coming, it's almost time for sleep.

The Butterfly

That day I remember when the butterfly
was expected, the whole city flooded down
to the harbour to wait and welcome, crowding
everywhere on the burnt, blackened wharves,
the crumbled docks and piers, climbing and fighting
to find a place from which the ocean, spread like a bat wing,
and the horizon could be seen. Toward noon
it appeared, a watered pink at first, a fleck
as of blood in saliva, fluttering crazily,
seeming not even to make toward us—and yet
it came on swiftly, spreading and rising up all at once,
a roaring orange veined with black, and blotted out
the sun. Between those fiery curtains, each
a hemisphere, the tube of worm was like
some cylindrical ship of living metal
where beings who had travelled from the stars
for centuries would peer out through ports
of black crystal…except that they were dead inside
and the sweet rot smell of carelessly preserved
entomological specimens filled the light.
Soon, though, it changed again, to Mourning Cloak,
to Tiger Swallowtail, to a humble yellow thing
that brought its own garden roiling under it
to replace the coal-tar waves. The sea was all spiked flowers,
goldenrod, lupin, loosestrife, delphinium,
and the butterfly stopped its anabasis our way
and got lost in the colours. We saw it hovering,
going on, nearer, farther, so frantic mad
with always more delight it could not pause
on any single crown. And then its female
came to it out of nowhere and the two tied a knot

in the air, and he stabbed his body into hers clinging
to a green translucent stem. A sparrow next,
a bird larger than an Africa of cloud
and yet demonically light and agile,
when they took flight, ate one of them
after a brief arabesque of dogfight. Was it our fly
that still lived? Then the hurricane—a little breeze that rose
when a spot darkened the sun—drove it tumbling
into the leaves. Torn petals
crowded the atmosphere, and whether its wings
of taut anile skin had been shattered and blown
with the flower fragments, or it had survived,
we couldn't see. It had dived like a fighter jet
going down into the jungle, hit,
behind a hill from which a moment later
comes up a plume of flame, but not a flame,
a burst of quiet came. And then our wait
seemed gone and we were watching
the black ocean again, congealed and trembling.

Your Story

Remember that you once lived, that you were,
that you were someplace here (I almost added
"with us in our world" but that might not be so).
Remember you had a story, even if you never knew.
Someone saw or felt you
and had to decide, had to make up
a history of you, even if it was a lie:
that you were nothing and easily forgotten.
And so you were, and it was too,
he forgot, we all forgot you, and now
nobody knows that story that is always being
rewritten: just as it meant
to do, it vanished with you. Even if
the perfect police erased you, knocked at your
navel or sex or the space between
with ceramic knuckle and wooden stock and slammed
through your flimsy door and scraped you
from your bed, and took you
and so you were warehoused—small
change of bones—with crawfish claws and mouse teeth
nowhere but in my charnel would-be
carnal words, nevertheless
remember. Even as I
command you this, I know
you don't. There's nothing to remember
and no one to remember it except
all of you unknown equally
in my voice or anywhere.

Place

A place belongs to the one who has most deeply
loved it, they said, has hoped in it beyond
its self-corruption. The land, people, the city

is his if his nights are for recalling it,
calling it in tears of aloneness and amazed
thanksgiving: that luck let him kiss it in his childhood,

that it grew into him, is him, that he still wants
to have it, save it, he wonders what it knows
tonight, right now, how it is with that place,

if it's happy, dying, dead. So he went back
carrying his book of that city: a great book,
yet only a dim sketch of his memory,

though in its pages, closed and dark, the alleys
of cracked windows and lintels, and children's paths
through towering weeds behind the empty stores

and under sycamores down to the river, burn
with bright emptiness that in the city were full of dust,
discarded bottles, concrete crumbs, and rusted

shavings in broken light. He did not have
a dollar in that place. He could not find
a door to open. He did not know a soul.

Better Days

Never anymore in a wash of sweetness and awe
does the summer I was seventeen come back
to mind against my will, like a bird crossing

my vision. Summer of moist nights full of girls
and boys ripened, holy drunkenness and violation
of the comic boundaries, defiances that never

failed or brought disaster. Days on the backs
and in the breath of horses, between rivers
and pools that reflected the cicadas' whine,

enervation and strength creeping in smooth waves
over muscular water. All those things accepted,
once, with unnoticing hunger, as an infant

accepts the nipple, never come back to mind
against the will. What comes unsummoned now,
blotting out every other thought and image,

is a part of the past not so deep or far away:
the time of poverty, of struggle to find means
not hateful—the muddy seedtime of early manhood.

What returns are those moments in the diner
night after night with each night's one cup of coffee,
watching an old man, who always at the same hour

came in and smiled, ordered a tea and opened
his drawing pad. What did he fill it with?
And where's he gone? Those days, that studious worker,

hand moving and eyes eager in the sour light,
that artist always in the same worn-out suit,
are my nostalgia now. That old man comes back,

the friend I saw each day and never spoke to,
because I hoped soon to disappear from there,
as I have disappeared, into the heaven of better days.

You That I Loved

You that I loved all my life long,
you are not the one.
You that I followed, my line or path or way,
that I followed singing, and you
earth and air of the world the way went through,
and you who stood around it so it could be
the way, you forests and cities,
you deer and opossums struck by the lonely hunter
and left decaying, you paralyzed obese ones
who sat on a falling porch in a deep green holler
and observed me, your bald dog barking,
as I stumbled past in a hurry along my line,
you are not the one. But you
are the one, you that I loved all my life long,
you I still love so in my dying mind
I grasp me loving you when we are gone.
You are the one, you path or way or line
that winds beside the house where she and I live on,
still longing though long gone
for the health of all forests and cities,
and one day to visit them,
one day be rich and free enough to go and see
the restricted wonders of the earth.
And you are the one, old ladies fated from birth
to ugliness, obesity and dearth,
who sat beside my path
one day as I flashed by. And you are the one,
all tumble-down shacks in disregarded hills
and animals the car on the road kills
and leaves stinking in the sun.

Childish Willow

I will let the tree stand
for many things they took away:
they cut you down, willow, my pavilion
of childhood, your leaves
were other birds and fish than those we know
in the streams and the air, another veil
of appearances around us, infant and naked
company, your height and spread another sky
that would admit the first and higher sky,
the blue one, through little gaps, as a guest.
They deprived me of you and locked me
screaming in my room until
your excision should be over,
and waited for time, which erases everything,
to calm me down and here I sit
decades later, maybe eons, I don't know,
like a smudged paper rubbed
to brittle thinness. The former marks on it
indeed are gone, almost, but the slightest stroke
would now tear through, so nothing
ever is written there. But surely it's evil
to stay a blank like this,
now that I'm grown and could destroy them,
evil to lie rubbed thin and yet untorn,
not to recut the faint scars,
and ooze, and howl.

What We Had

I really did love you in a sense, colleagues,
friends and fellow citizens and passersby
of my day here, who stormed the smoking world,
struggling to plant your flags or at least be heard.
I looked at you with consistent and unfeigned
interest, delighted in the revelation
of your pointless variety. It was joy to know
myself a poet among so many who knew
it also, but kept it quiet—the one thing
you did keep quiet. So many males and females
of divers pretensions: fortified handmade heights
from which in rage and fear you each would look
downward at me and melt in love. And I
would melt too and would feel the sympathy
of living with you among the flowers and rocks,
and dream sometimes for long seconds on end
that all any of you wanted was blessèd life
for everyone, and me too. But she and I
clung to each other, comrades, and I understood
that you more truly were the storm, and though
the two of us are dead now, what we had
to do in life, in fact, was to survive you.

Tragic Vision and Beyond

Is that the full moon and its dark bruise-like markings,
or the shadow of a man in a slouch hat with crumpled brim
looking in at our blackness through a round window
beyond which lies a flat buckwheat-flour light?
There's really no question: simply, the one it is
"looks like," "reminds me of" the one it's not.
It's as though some great hunter who was also a great singer
sang: "I lay in wait all of a night and a day and a night
for the young deer to move, trying not to fall into a dream
of her sweet fat. Then I could wait no longer:
was she a demon, never blinking, stiller than a rock?
I notched my arrow and crept up, waiting for her to bound
beyond me, tasting the disappointment to come
if she should sniff me too soon. But she
never stirred and I came close enough to grab her heart
in my fist. She was just shadow among the tree trunks
and all my strength against sleep had been for nothing.
I was asleep and dreaming from the start. I the hunter
was a dream my hunger had, a dead stock standing in the forest
a night and a day and a night." And his song was deeply loved,
the most intoxicating song, but now there's no one left
who knows it because his whole race, all twenty of the people,
died the end of that summer in the drought.

The Tidal Wave

One day I'll wake and see the tidal wave above my city
fulgurating at its dripping diamond crest in the sun
like another, a nearer, sun, and its sheer wall
under its beautiful crown of spume will be
a vertical plain wider than any on earth, a bare steppe
but of flesh, flesh of planed and planished liquid
teak and jet and jade.
How tall will it be—three miles, a hundred miles? How far
or imminent? Will there be seconds or years
before it falls on us? I only know it won't matter anymore
that I was sick in mind. Under the shadow or in the light
of the wave I remembered childhood,
when I dewinged a moth, inspected
the writhing tube and then forgot, went elsewhere.
And manhood, when the memory came back one day
twenty years later and so I couldn't reach the moth
to give the gift of murder, impose release
on its horror as the pure ignorance
of my imagination created it
and felt it. This I thought of every day and hour
to the exclusion of battling like everyone
with everyone for the bread reserved
to others. I slipped into alley mouths
and doorways among empty buildings and occupied
myself all day with saying my nightly prayers, O God
please take away the carcinoma, aphasia, ataxia,
the monomania, hysteria, dementia from her
and him, the age from them, aren't they old
enough already, why should they have to get
still older, till the list of them
became so long that many died

as I forgot them, as my day
became not long enough to run through the vast roll
and pronounce it all. I lost
who they were in the bourdon of their names
rumbling in me, shaking the frame
till I thought my ears were bleeding and I clawed
my skull—but nothing was happening there, in fact I,
the face that faced it, looked roseate, glimpsed
in dark windows, and cheerful. A conscious eminence
absorbed in guilt and supplication, scraggy psalms,
while the citizens ran on and soon forgot
the ones at the gate fallen
with broken leg and twisted bowels and waiting and hoping
to be shot. But when the wave appears
above the city, all this will proceed as usual,
it's what we know, and the absolute equality
of what I do and what they do, my strength and theirs,
will appear in the water's black and crystal glow.

The Sentinel

The one who watches while the others sleep
does not see. It is hoped, it is to be hoped
there is nothing to see. The camp has quieted
behind him and all is peace there—let it be—
at his back, where he longs to turn his face
and see the walls of pitched cloth that hide
his comrades, sleeping. But lights go down, and out,
and if he turned there would be nothing, black,
with just the bulks of looming tents aglow
with just the memory of last evening's light.
Likewise, nothing to see in the outward
dark before his face, where there is nothing,
it is to be hoped—only a darkness
of useless vigilance, unless it is a darkness
of hostile conniving lights not lit out there,
surrounding treachery, faces smeared with ash
to blend in with the night and lying low.
And what if morning ever comes, when things
are just as always, it's obvious to all?
Won't he have to find some commander and report
everything he observed? Out and beyond
the perimeter, he notes nothing that may not be
a moth fluttering or a shooting star
behind thick cloud. Within the camp, though,
constant stirrings. Sudden snorts as if breath
cut off by some torturer was suddenly permitted,
the hands unclenched from the throat at the last
second before death. And longer, steady snores,
woodmen in snowy forests. Whimpers of mothers'
and pet dogs' names, uncertain breezes moist
with tears and snot fluttering the tent flaps,

men curled up knees to nose and heels to hips
like ringed camps and feeling only
the anus's openness and the back a target,
or stretched out straight, cupping and tangling fingers
in hair and cooing to the genitals as if
to a girlfriend. Fart, belch, and vomit,
urine, dirt, and sperm falling in latrines,
shuffle of feet on stones, books, letters, pictures
felt for under brittle pillows and the dreams
of bleeding inwardly, of growing a third arm,
of removing the penis like a banana from its skin
and passing it around the campfire, vaguely anxious
the others won't pass it back. But
the commanders, wouldn't they tell him:
What good's this report? You saw nothing
you were supposed to see. You wasted your time
listening to us, but we knew where we were
and what was going on here. And you saw only
the obvious and trivial and drew the worst conclusions.
Or drew no conclusions, it's simply that the obvious
always looks filthy: any obstruction you can't pass
or at least see through takes the form to you
of a rotting cellar wall aswarm with worms.
Besides, none of this ever happened. You
made it up to humiliate us, you are a foreign
agent, which is why no hint of the enemy's
numbers, movements, or power ever appears
anywhere in your lying reports. You fell asleep
at your sacred post and this report records
your evil dreams, a spontaneous creation you love
and so a deeper shame to you than if
you had rationally constructed out of sheer depravity
this libel on your comrades. And who
appointed you at all? You are not the sentinel.

The sentinel has already given his intelligence,
which we are analyzing. You are the lonely watcher,
the one who won't sleep until it's time to work,
the one who wants a salary and a title
for insomnia. If we have nightmares,
it's that we hear your footsteps under our window,
wake up, look out along the street: no one.
That's what they'll say. And yet the report
will have to be filed, the storm endured. But not till dawn.
It is almost possible, it would almost be possible
to enjoy this fogged-in darkness, this dewfall and
rustling silence, the accustomed expectation
of receiving the first shot if indeed the enemy
has chosen tonight, except that one can't relax,
each detail must be noted or the report
will be a lie. In fact through no fault of his own
the sentinel will miss something, and the report
he contemplates, or the refusal to report
he also contemplates, will be a traitorous lie.
To light a match might well draw fire. He strikes,
it doesn't catch. But no, it sputters, waits,
then flares. He moves it to his lips, and peace.

Cleanliness

Dead flies on the windowsills, the corpses now
of more than one summer, weightless but unstirred,
on the third story at the top of the stairs.

Impossible for her to climb them now.
Too much tiredness. But she will still
go there again someday, she promises.

Will rest the bucket and sponge on every step
and breathe, waiting for the water to stop
sloshing in the pail and her heart to stop beating.

Even if every step's an hour, a threat of death,
the attic will be clean again. We watch.
We notice the streaked tableware, the dust,

chipped things, and flecks of old food lying here,
on this first floor, its clearly dirty windows
beyond the ladder of her eyes, while in her words,

in her thought, only the lament goes on
for the space above, that it's filling up with webs,
that its contents, our pasts, are waiting to be given

or thrown away. And how much we'd give now
for the oppressive cleanliness that once
reached every day, angrily, into the least

and darkest corners of our childhood
to show us its vigour again, that fearful
enemy we won our best days in opposing.

Arrogance

They easily recognized the reprehensible arrogance
of the poet vilifying "a whole population
that goes about its business and doesn't know
it is no longer human." They on the other hand
valued common things: a day at work at a screen or a window,
noon in sunny streets, bright signs, the office girls
showing their legs as they ate sitting on concrete banks
in the plaza by city hall. They acknowledged that to walk
at such times past the form lying against a wall,
wrapped with thick blankets despite torturing humidity,
shamed them and assured them they were alive. Too vague
a claim, they admitted, doubling back honestly on themselves,
vague as a billboard: I am alive. So trying to be clear
and fair, they felt like passengers who believe
when they are told it won't be so bad up ahead
where the crowded train is taking them,
it will be worth the long journey herded
offensively close with many others, developing for a few
who happen to be jammed nearby a necessary,
compensatory love. It won't be so bad. It will even
be better. After all, each stage of the journey
so far has been tolerable: maybe
the seeming steady decay in conditions is in truth
only aging, a tendency to discomfort
and querulousness, one of the common things,
decline of their capacity to endure.

The Moment

It is the moment when something must be done
and in this it is like every other moment
and one is ignoring it
and in this it is like every other moment
and it has disappeared without disaster, benefit, or trace
and in this it is like every other moment.
And one doesn't know if the tingling in the legs is a mortal disease
just making its first showing, or fear.
It is the moment when something must be done
but the telephone rings in a fire station down by the distant lake
and a blimp passes above a man training dogs in a narrow back yard
and a screen door slams adding the final drop that makes nervousness
overbrim miles away and run down the hot black street.
Also a desultory guitar gets sick for the moment and drags
the fingers of the picker into a definite illness
and also wilted daisies are brought home from a store because they
were cheap
and are stuck in some water but nothing will revive them
but there they are, beautiful nonetheless and dropping gold
and purple petals all over a yellowing
paperback copy of *And Then There Were None*,
but the culprit slinks away drenched in a sudden brilliant storm
that has arisen to prevent the detective from reading to the end.
The moment has come when one must go to bed
and quench the ever-intensifying restlessness in darkness.
Otherwise it will catch fire and be day again,
there will be no more darkness, no more rest,
and in this it will be like every other moment.

Sound of Hungry Animals

There was a sound of hungry animals at night
or animals in the pain of their coitus
or the self-hatred of their inseparable pack
grieving, and beneath my conscious prayer
in the relief of the cool and humid darkness
the one spirit spoke betraying my desire
for some good of which I could never be aware.

Poem of Courtly Love

I want to hate what is believed: that darkness
is first and silence best, that the good part
of the word is wind, and the adequate part
an image, that the chance part is the beginning
and the necessary part the end. I want
to sit with you, unable to understand
the book that holds all human story to be
an allegory of our dying
proposals of rebirth. I want this book
we were reading to slip from your lap
as you tremble, seeking courage to surrender,
so the interpretations woven insidiously into plot lines
lie face down in dust, and the story
that starts with your breast
opens in our air—nipples, eyes, tongues,
and the words to come
happy in the pause
that is their natural home.

The Red Car

Little red car in which I saw them drive away,
boy and girl with their curious striped cat in his cage,
with my map of the way to Michigan, ancient map
that shows Big Beaver Road and Bloomfield Hills
already lost in the wilds of Detroit, no bloom,
no field, no beaver, be the car I dreamed.
Be the little red MG I want for my wife.
You're only a rented pocket sedan, but be
that sportscar of a dire adventure that never fails.
This is the best of life, this instant, these years
of loving them on the edge of a black cliff
where their falling would turn the green earth to an ash,
to a mummy's lips, while it went on twinkling,
brushing my breast with its orange hair as if nothing
had changed. And what would have changed? Many
have died in the space of these lines. But little red car,
carry them safe and I will carry you safe.
I'll love you forever, as we say, my friend,
knowing perfectly
that memory and body disappear,
identifying ourselves with the long drive to reappearance.

Two Crickets

Cool darkness and no peace. In the room's black,
the ceiling swarms with smears of light cast out
from open eyes. Images never quite images,
parts of bodies yet to coalesce
in an always future hell. Outside, one cricket
singing with long still pauses—August is over.
And for the moment no one harries him
or pecks him up, he doesn't despise his own invention,
doesn't worry the song of longing he repeats
is ignorant, failing to know and bring all things
the wise and passionate will ever say of love
to his lady. Listen and you seem to be in his peace
under the leaves of an impatiens flower.
There's dew all over your body and a slight stir
fans it to further cold but you don't shiver. Who knows?
August is over, for the moment no one harries
or eats us, we sing stupidly free of doubt.

Bewilderment

I love the bewilderment of God
when looking at you he wonders:
It was for her I created all the rest,

women, and men, and the animals,
and everything that, to underlie them,
had to exist—crystals, elements, forces—

and all that had to wait, showing the way
ahead and above: gods and demons,
prophets, gnostics, the All and Nothing,

the darkness before I am and which I built
as a bed. But was everything for her?
I wonder, because when I saw her

and in that first excitement invented wheat,
and reaped, threshed, milled, mixed, kneaded,
and baked, and tested the bread with my mouth

and my nose, each loaf, so that somewhere
in the succession from my oven and hand
she would occur, I had to devour every one.

They were all equal, perfect
copies of her, each different, differently
to be consumed. And I

determined to go on forever,
both before her lifetime and forever after,
producing her. But what's gone wrong?

Why won't they give her what she needs,
or give themselves what they all need,
when it's lying there in the world

where I put it, at her feet: just let
her be. Quit crimping, marching her,
demanding obedience. Let her follow

that law I read for the first time
when I thought her, when I heard her
reasoning freely by the rule she is.

But no: she's there in the middle
of their cities and ages, and all around her
are others all wrong. Whenever

he sees you this way incomparable on earth
then I love you, suddenly know you, call you
bewilderment of God come here.

Her Work

I love to see you draw the hammer back.
It pauses there up in the air, a bird behind your ear
hovering to survey a vast country for one spot,
and it shines silver as light undercuts and buoys it
and my face shines too, reflecting its weighty
and polished determination pocked
with little flaws—now I feel them in my skin:
scars, dints of earlier strikes, or openings
for senses that want to be much deeper than they are
but still see only what's before them. The claw
scrolls out, is wind made stainless steel,
a breeze of someone's being about to run so freely
the mere intention lifts and curves his hair
into an ancient image of future power.
The wooden handle stabs the steel and the head
clutches the wood and your hand at the apogee
moves just a little without moving at all,
like upper reaches of a still tree, but the angles
at wrist and elbow, the distortion of the shoulder
are there now to vanish, stand in a forest
of vanishings: you bring the hammer down.

To the Still Unborn

You don't know me but I was once watching films and films
of yet another man-caused horror germinating in the depths.
I was sitting alone with a television's loud images of fear,
repetitious and badly made. I was wondering why
I couldn't turn them off. Always an outpost, a small
and stupid crew in some corner of sea floor, void, or desert,
was being assaulted by a beast that enters the human body
and turns it first to a monster bubbling in pain,
then finally to a blank, viscid, and implacable enemy:
image of the human self-experiment. Or rather, this image
as it appears to the hucksters who made these awful movies
and sold them to my nights, otherwise quiet in the hum
of refrigerator engine and whistle of aural nerves decaying.
I wondered why I didn't turn them off and think of you,
didn't pierce through fear of the great strain it would be
to compose my mind's noise, my senses' palsy
the way hands can be folded or legs formed into a root,
the sort of root a canoe's hull or the belly of a tern
offers to water, moving on its own pressure and soft shadow.
Was I hopeless because you were never thinking of me?
But you didn't yet exist then, when I was sitting in my kitchen,
hoping soon to turn off the companionable horror of my day
and think of you, quiet, powerful, come from the future
rescuing me not as I imagined you but as you will be.

The Sun

My sun, I see your colour fall
again on everything on earth. The trees
are lifted out of darkness,
and there are flowers,
people (they talk), and houses that create
warm spaces in the great
night and the cold, waiting for you,
almost in despair, their powers
fading. These all spring up
from dimness to full life again
because of you, as if they were no more
than low reliefs carved badly in black slate
until you shine. Then their true bodies
open as desert plants
rise when rare rainfall brings to sudden birth
brief spring, insane and joyful:
plants that break only once through covering earth,
as if young men and women opened
flat gravestones, and walked out
by the same entranceway the terrifying corpses
yesterday and years ago
went in.

PART V

2012–2015

The Book to Come

Each page in this book is first. Each re-begins
everything the others had decided
once and for all—"Behold, I make all things new"—
and happy, forgets the others
ever were. It sets out at naked dawn
in culpable but perfect innocence,
joys in the terror of stumbling on alone,
grows sick of the perpetual recurrence,
eternal return to childhood,
the endless concourse of fresh days: nothing
but uninhabited wealth and being free
and needing to make it a world. Each longs to be
one worker among many, a happy piece
in a progress—longs for a mature
continuity, a classic harmony of measured
stages completed and preserved, dross purged
and the pure sums added, the clear results
amounting to a city held in a single glance.
In that splendid extent each page trudges lost
and when it stumbles, startled it comes on words
of another there before it—"Breathing in,
breathing out, o Elysium"—and sees
its hope is wrong, its glory dark, and so
crosses itself out and starts again.

Simplicity

The first and simplest things were best.
Light, and then darkness and wind.
Water, which is light with darkness
for its body and wind
for its blood and action. Then trees
arise on its banks: complex things
and implying complexities, implying
a whole earth, but staying where they are,
at home to pay homage to the simple.
Trees arise and are unformed song,
whether sound when the air stirs
or the rhythm of their standing side by side
in silent black or bright. Next comes one
travelling, eager, a dread of what comes next,
who stops under them awhile,
imagines their lyrics, and imagines
himself abolished in simplicity.

The Location of the World

I think that in the interstices
in my sobriety, an expanse
like a humid night with lightning
or a dry poisoned ground or a concrete wall
and their veins of narrow cracks,
I am almost insane. And that madness
is a cool summer rarely recalled
or a cool episode of an unbearable summer, one night
where the light of the west delayed under the oaks
and spread through your hair and eyes and around your temples,
not wanting to descend from there
even into the valley of the moon
and its transformations. A time, a flower
too tiny to be known to anyone—
when I ask its name, there's a blank
silence and I too forget I ever had it
in my eyes, almost my hands,
growing from the rare fissures.

The Snake

When you said no to me I lived two years in hell
and then came out again and walked the streets like anyone,
disproving the doctrine that the inferno's closed,
no redemption there. It has an open door of passing time
but the resurrected carry it inside as fading scar
and predestined resting place. So it was for the snake in Eden.
The hideous one became this snake, leaving hell behind
to crawl in flowering grasses, gleam on granite shelves,
sleep in a grotto, go out and sip a spring
fresh as the first dawn, which happened every day,
and not even waylay the rabbit, for this was Eden,
before the time when there was any need. It's good
to be a snake, to feel your firm length and thickness
under the purring, licking sun, to feel your body write
an S across the loam and not know there is "S"
in some realm of untouchable forms and painful
grasping and not grasping them yet to be invented.
To be all agility, muscle robed in its own power
taking on flesh of rose and gold brocade. To breathe
and split your hide and grow, keeping the same eyes,
but skinned now, with everything a greater glory that had seemed
supreme glory before—to keep your perpetual eyes
open, open all night, all day, and with your tongue
observe, enjoy the shapes and motions of heat
as a hawk sees valleys and ridges below him, as a god
watches the waves of centuries. It's good to be with your dry body
all around a human woman, your head erect and alert
before her sex, contemplating the darkness under the rosy
plumpness and light fur, like a warm stone with lichen,
thinking you could go in, while your coils—a hundred fingers
that are all one limb—stretch out between her hips,

around one thigh, across her back
to circle a breast and the neck, and your pointed tail
comes almost to rest in, almost to tickle, her navel.
It's good to be a snake, yet horrible too,
to have no arms, a mummy wrapped alive,
a man used to freedom, the shape of the human body,
but bound around now with heavy ropes
and left to lie for the coming of the torturer,
helpless forever, no hand to lift himself, to wave,
to push back pain—a cylindrical bulk
of cloud carried west, the furled withering tube
of a fallen hollyhock flower, a bowel torn out, pulsing...

The New Measures

Metropolis, great salt mother, don't be angry
we've left you, a hive
of empty paper cells exposed, a speckle
in the scream of the dry tree.
From up there you could see,
if you could see, and pity
our dewinged march in the new mud. If we
in fact are more than one now.
If we are even three, the man and the following
woman and their lugged child, maybe dead,
on the plain without feature. Depending on the strength
of the sucking ooze from spot to spot,
their feet fall lighter or heavier
and shifting cadences occur,
arousing memories that forbid but can't prevent
nostalgia: tempi of the marches
of great armies go on for three, four steps,
then fall into the pattern
of naked boys and girls—io! io!—
treading a dance at a wedding,
three or four steps, and next the thunder metre
of vast herds, then quickly a swinging stomp
of dosido-ers on a straw-dusted pine plank floor, the beat
of runners in stadia of mown grass,
the wedding dance again, an erotica, the armies,
feet on subway stairs, long pulses
of the strides of skaters...limping of wheels,
click, click-click of a paper clip dropped
and caught in the works of a fan, the wheeze-whistle
of loosening belts in old motors...brief riffs,
mordents, crushed notes, grace notes appearing,

winks of accent in the plod...
                              the last
of the hurl-burrl of the great city
that likening itself to a sea seemed
about to produce an inhuman music:
unvaryingly various, the surge and swell of our bodies
in unequal ranks breaking on each other,
lapsing together. To this we thought
we'd come the way we used to come to the shore
in the dark and pose our backs against
a cold fallen column of driftwood and listen
to the income and output of the ocean
in its bounds, at our feet—one who threatened
to destroy us and promised to continue
and so we were lulled
to power through those nights of ours
of sodden or dewy tiredness. But all of that broke
on the scurry of strait streets,
a wave, a dawn, an execution,
and I promise you, mother, we never did leave,
we love you,
it's simply that one morning we were gone.

The Volcano

This was the earth at last. The volcano
pluming in the distance, white at its lips
that etched a kiss's shape into the sky,
brown on its shoulders with dead lava,
green toward its base. To see it rise
brought back, wound and healing,
the presence of the anthill so long buried
in our memory: buried with our five-year-old
seeing that once admired it. We lay at the tree's base
and watched each moment in the come and go
of the red ants: the scissoring mandibles,
nervous antennae swivelling every way,
the dragged burdens of white wing-scraps, the crossed paths
of two or three, confusions, turnings back, small wars,
and the constant crumbling of the hill: tumblings
of pale gold grains, dislodged
by the workers' footfalls, down the slope
from the black hole at the summit all day long
absorbing and divulging ants.

       We recognized
then what we know: our earth today
fails to be earth, and yet in every touch
of my fingers and your hair, childhood's touch
in grass and shade still feels itself, so yes,
today is still the earth. And now we're there again
with everyone we remember. In the weakness
of the men and women of today
we remember not many: back to our grandmother,
no farther. But she's with us, she remembers
her grandfather, so he's there too, and his

grandmother, since he recalls her. And she
recalls her mother, and what makes us laugh,
now we recall her too—her lap, the shadow
of her breasts, her clothes and colours, and the soil,
roots and stems, the stamens and pollen of the flowers
of her scent. Then, dead two hundred years
in our delusion, she kisses us and says, "Children,
this is my father, you've never met him,
I haven't seen him in a long long time."

Eve

The freedom of imagination is
a matter of the weather—the inner
and the outer weather. Is it possible
to sing of summer in the winter,
spring in autumn? Your beard
and brows encased in wind-born ice, your face
a vanished race's famous statue…
to look at the three sparrows plumped and shivering
in a cedar bush, sole and rifled cottage
against the horizontal howl,
fails to reveal if in their hearts is the image
of a better time or only the ongoing
of an engine not yet off. The prayers
of Eve, who once talked with God, are similar.
She who went naked through the day and night,
inspired a lust that was the pith of cleanness,
bathed in the river and the seeing of the sun,
patted the phallus eels and fishes
and the tiger's nose, her shut-up
house now stinks of her urine, she can't smell it,
can't taste, can hardly hear, moans out
her son's name, "Abel. Abel. Abel,"
till the old man comes halting
with ruined back to try to lift
and clean her. It would be better, he thinks,
right now to be being murdered
out in the clear air, an unseen blow
and darkness, freedom, as my smoke ascends
among the timothy, in the summer scent.
My brother, where are you to share
my burden, my mother? And he went through

this and later died wifeless,
dupe of a pornographic dream, a girl
naked all the day and night. His grave is there
under the high chain-link topped with barbed wire
that runs endlessly across that lush
empty country, where on the other side
metal has never been, will never be discovered.
The overgrowth of wild grape vines,
junk trees, and milkweed makes the fence
a perfect screen and beyond it
he sited the parkland where she played.

Voice as Time, World, and Presence

When the last page of the scriptures
blows down the street, watched by sausage strings, rust-coloured
    fedoras,
and sunset glints in broken glass...When it blows along
accompanied by page seven of a newspaper
from thirteen years ago, school levy narrowly defeated...
When they skitter together but apart
like two dogs, nosing into corners, sticking,
then running on...Was the last page
torn out in despairing anger or saved to cling to, to hold
next to a heart, before an eyeball? Did the last man
cherish it, spit on it, or is it a random ash, from when he went out
on his back lawn to read the holy book and the funnies
in shades and shorts, at ease on his chaise longue
of aluminum tubing and plastic upholstery, ready to receive
a tan from the bomb burst before the blast wave approached
and his body exploded like a dry tree when a wildfire
creeps close down a slope? In any case, Lord,
put an arm around my shoulder, now that I'm alone.
Let me feel your hand, see your eyes. Don't tell me
if I need a sign I'm a faithless generation. No question
of faith remains. I'm alone. I need your voice
human in my human ear, the way I heard
my lover's words. Not a story to be recalled
but a story continued day by day ever varied:
the heaven of her wisdom I would try, I swore,
to remember forever. Then she was gone and it faded
day by day. Her words, her ideas gone, only the tone
of love remaining. And then the tone too gone.
Only a sense we had talked once day by day,
a knowledge of heaven stretching back to the dawn

of my earth. Although destroyed it remained,
a beautiful homeland if only I could reach it.
A conversation, the hearing of the clear voice
of another once in the cool air, words that became,
it's true, a legend later when they faded,
but the voice never: now and always it went on.

Farewell to Lake Michigan

Put your hand into my side, the oak said,
the full moon in his May crown. My love and I were leaving
the shore of Lake Michigan as a home forever
although we swore we'd come again
over and over, wraiths in the paths where strangely
we would not meet ourselves—as if belovèd
returnings for years had failed to carve our mark there
deeply enough. I'd gone out to the bluff
to visit the oak a final time, my friend,
in his pride of place in Olmstead's paradise
along and above the monster of frigid energy,
paradise itself for the invulnerable eye to play in
immensity and change. I circled him. My hands
were on his bark, my eyes in his filtered light
from lamps along the path and from the moon,
my thought part with him and part polluted
with Druids and the groves of Dodona, but trying
to be pure of knowledge. As if I could memorize
his form and body in my spine, so the image
of my skeleton and nerves would branch and leaf in me
and my body blossom in the world. Was this,
it struck me, the return of cryptic mysticism,
or a radical democracy, tree and man free equals?
Then: "A rebirth of mysticism," he said,
"is the one way to a complete equality."
This is just my translation of light and shadow
along his trunk, the subtle panoply
of his night greys, the cold roughness of his skin
on my hands: the words of his inner mass, the flow
he's carved in. But an accurate translation.

Essential Poem

for John Hollander

Although it's likely you're on your own
(at this moment in this city of five million)
reading the poems of Traherne,
and there was no one till you lit your lamp,
the kingdom of childhood keeps being founded
in his voice and his seeing,
which are a sort of birth. A birth goes on
in the dark of a poor family, or a mother alone.
Then comes the small bright circle of the faces:
lover pores over sleeping loved one, parent over child
in their enclosure we name home,
a hut in the plain so bare there's not a tongue
of grass to make the wind hiss. Unknown
to the world a world exists:
trees and streams, birds all the colours of the flowers.
So Traherne pours over you
his wild remembrance of the world to come. And would
even in the silence of his book
if it were lost and lay unopened
two hundred years. Even if he had died
before he sang the Eden in his look.

The Good Listener

How often I've heard him tear himself apart
in front of me, and what was beautiful
was miserable. As in my nursing work I see
the insides of a head sometimes — like a pumpkin,
they always say, kicked and breached, the wet
pulpy meat, sticky and sickly sweet-smelling,
the lumpy slurry with its pips and fibres:
all that remains of complicated dreams
that were continuous somehow with hope:
next year's vine. Or a body is being cut
open and I help. It's hard to do, thank God,
preoccupying, because without the strain,
the horror of the wet machine behind the smooth
belly now turned to a flap would... Who made him
be so in pain inside, tangled in himself
and hating the knot, that again and again he rips
his quiet face off? It's like the shrieks and sobs
of a marriage coming out from behind a still
house front, out the windows, across the garden
and into the street, a mean gang of noises,
pathetic bullies, forcing everyone else
to cower under them — does that comfort him?
It seems as though there has to be a play
and there's nothing else he has to put on stage.
Just what's inside, but it's ugly. Ugly when
let out into the light, like a bowel or heart.
At first I felt compassion but I can't live
with my love brought down to compassion.
The image of a man as strength, a beautiful
skin over a fire, is a necessary world
even if only an image desired so much

it's worse than needed. Now that my world
has been destroyed, I'll have to find another.

The Visible Brother

In the prison
house of my imagination
imagination is the prisoner and inmate,
desperate, comfortable,
and imagination is the wall, the one
landscape the inmate has ever known,
and windows in the wall that show
a deep valley and the endless
revolving sky. Or are those pictures?
Moving pictures, which only means
they move us, not that there's motion there
although I feel you with me, invisible brother
who never speaks, as I walk across the field
at November's end, first day I see
every last leaf is down. On my entering
the park: a man, a poor half-cracked
man known to me by sight, confronting,
almost kissing, the smooth clear orange bark
of a naked tree. Head way back in neck-breaking
throat-proffered-to-the-murderer position,
he watches a black squirrel, glossy as a star,
in a high groin, rummaging
through the white sky. He has a friend,
oblivious, this creature. I am walking
to the doctor, maybe to the entrance
to the passage to death,
still passage in the shape
of a body outstretched between dreaming and pain,
where you withholding the power that I want
will sit by me
unknown to me and weep.

Painting and Poem

Time had to be mined from the painting, the delusion
of stillness was so powerful in it.
Gem or magma, motion was frozen up,
enthralled, below its surface: the two friends
in a mild late summer evening. Their hands
have just quit touching. One of them will go
in a white skiff at their feet, out past the headland
with its cylindrical temple in the middle distance.
The woman they both love is not portrayed
except as the golden sunrise or more likely
sunset to which all lines recede, the mouth
of shadow spilling light for now. Also the light
comes from them, is the fount of their eyes and sex
turning to the west. I had to read the painting
a long time to see the poem it entraps,
trying to redeem words from fury and long time.
First I imagined it hung on a wall in a train
racing to collision decade after decade
till it became antique. The wood of the old coach
and the ties rotted, the engine and the rails
rusted, the railroad slumped into earth, the painting
remained alone hurtling ahead, a tattered
scrap of bygone taste. And why imagine a train,
I thought next. Just by hanging in the world
the painting's on that train. Its mild regretful
stasis of a perfect dying afternoon,
warm, dry, and soft, in a rich temperate land
that everyone remembers, even if he's never known it—
it's so much like those pauses where the struggle
to prosper, or survive, doesn't matter, as if we had died
and judgement had been in our favour, we'll be allowed

to re-begin our failed attempts forever
without injury, in hope. All this is plunging
into the blank forward. An invisible haste,
an unvarying acceleration, carries it
whether to wreck or wear away in the wind
who knows? And that's why there's nothing mild
beneath the image. Words scream out. A wound
of sound thickens but oozes, never quite
scarring over, or a knife too quick to be seen
re-cuts it, and it springs again. And someone
comes to stand before this over and over
and fastens the word beautiful to the fact.

News

They brought him news: the serpent had come
from its hole in the golden mud and stung
and killed his wife beside the river
as she was bathing. They came running
through the fields, tunnelling the high gold hay,
making a ripple—like a breeze
or the flowing mark of a hidden snake,
its advance in the grass—which he had seen
when they were still far off. He looked
homeward from his work under his vines,
his hands still raised among the grapes
as if he were tied, they later said,
to be beaten there. His head was twisted
to his left shoulder and tipped back slightly
to lift the gaze, and the sky was cut out
by the line of his nose, lips, and chin—
a complex coast, blue sea, white shore—
and they thought of how the corpse was lying
waiting for him, naked, wet
with river as though with dew, its profile
against the dim of the hut and the rush mat.

His vines were savage, yet the sweetest.
He grew the wild grape unimproved.
Now his grainy fingers in the bunches
of the small violet dusty fruits
were like pale goldenrods gone to seed
mixed in among October asters...
but in these grapes, like a loud cry
heard once in the night so sharp and clear
that when it's gone it's not believed

by the only one who heard it, was sweetness
that made the farmers drink their envy
and strain against heaven's injustice
and feel now in their fatal news,
in their duty, a hateful satisfaction.

Then he ran home and running he saw
a walnut lying withered far
from any walnut tree, and faded,
hardly green, so that he thought it
a horse's dropping at first, but then
a walnut. He saw the pine cones, some
smashed, some perfectly unfolded.
The brown suns of the chestnuts, some
nibbled, the green-white innards bared.
He saw a mushroom, grey and crossed
by wide white causeways, and another
kicked over—saw the jagged stump
of the stem, a broken world of breakings,
like the young mountains are. He came
to the hut, bent down to the low door,
dark and small, and she received him,
happy to see him. She kissed him, the full
length of her stripped body kissed him,
the front and the back of her body kissed him
all at once. Then they went out,
forgot she was naked from the bathing,
from that interrupted making ready,
forgot the grapes too, and walked together
by the river, back the way the screams
of the women had come, into the hay
where the silent messengers had gone,
and tried to remember and tell each other
their whole day, all that they'd seen and done.

In the Dead of Night Only

It's in the dead
of night only
that you wake up—
in the dark between the stars and the sun,
night exhausted, dawn not yet.

Only then is attention real, godlike. Then it sees
how far it is from being god. It sees
in a darkness blacker than the young night's
beautiful colour, known at last
now in nostalgia. A blackness darker
than light in pure space.

Then you recognize
the journey in which your bed is an evening's pause:
it's the house of this moment
in which the journey is a dream.

The Caravan of the Merchants

The caravans of the merchants, Valente writes,
Las caravanas de los mercaderes,
and I wonder, look up in wonder at the street.
And does it matter that the merchant's caravans
are trucks? Huge tractors — Freightliner, Peterbilt,
International, Western Star — and giant cartons
with lettuces and cornucopias of loaves
painted two stories high along their sides.
Big-screen stills from a movie of abundance,
signs of the wealth being
hauled to us, threatening to fall over, to crush us
like a comber, a leaning wall, as the truck strains
to bend around a right-angle corner
and we step back. And think of Anaïs Nin
all at once knowing herself woman, small,
as she walked next to passing truck tires
twice her height. Of Juan Ramón: in childhood
he saw three oxen taller at the shoulder
than the highest roof tiles of the village. Giant
oxen of life and vision: this world is another.
I think of a boy in Babylon lying on his bed,
calm but vibrating in aftermath pleasure,
just having come from his friends, their jokes,
their easy strength. Never again, he thinks
in exultation, will a moment be like ours:
this style of grace, the subtle transformations
ours alone in this incomparable language
that we make with every expedition for love
with the girls, our happy prodding, their happy
defiance. A moment supreme till time ends.
A moment of a world, our youth, our invention,

constant, condensed in a song, and always
living in a next moment, another day. Never
was there in the world nor will there be
this agile splendour and flow. He swells
(as our saying goes) with pride, and looking up
at the cars, backpacks, cellphones, and the trucks
of the merchants, I agree with him, I am him.

An Ancient Man

I am a modern man,
this that goes along in the guise of a member of a salt-route
    caravan.
Or in the guise of not even a man at all,
a mollusc from when this desert was a sea
that insists with its creeping that its world remains
somewhere in the dry air.

I'm a modern man and insist on the body.
All transfiguration comes in the body
and partakes of sickness, the itch, the wash of crying
    chemicals,
the world's flesh-eating schedules, the steps of sunset.
Of needing to endure the unendurable separation.
Struggling to wake again bright every moment in this bed.

But I feel my face and see the dunes:
low heaps with lax slopes
like cheeks, jowls, and forehead sifting away.
So don't tell me the bones are not a jail for the spirit.
I'll die in these bones that will remain unchanged
even when they're nothing. I am an ancient man.

The Last Garden

We yearned to grow down and back
to the child. We called the child
fruit, flower, and reason of the human.
We said the long afterward, our life...we possess it merely
so that the child at its beginning can be:

the aching care for the child
to give it its paradise, trying to last for that task,
the care to contradict the withering of our muscles,
the falling apart of our bones, falling asleep
of our nerves, our needs, their glamour—this struggle
     only exists
because it must for the child, its beginning, to be.

We said, "I have had my paradise."

Evil dreams. The child a wanderer through
the desert of them
into ruined adolescence, the last garden.

The voice of the prophet came to us like the squeaking
of a bat receding in the night:
I am more than eighty years old...
what bloom is this more than the bloom of youth...
beauty that descends on me and rises out of me...
O if I could only return to the house where I was born
and hear the birds, the same birds
that were my friends then, sing once more.

We heard the voice rustling, remembered only now, in the ear
of our childhood's end: Woe to you

who are rich,
you have had your consolation.

Under Green Trees Far Away

Under green trees far away
the splendour, the light over everything,
fills with shadows,
a voice, a gesture
answering another, excited hands and eyes
finding themselves
living.

These dead, who invented only death.

Far away under green trees what was hidden
in the folds of clothing, crotch, and brain glows
in faces of an unruined adolescence.

An Accidental Structure

An accidental structure:
she like you
could not have been,
but there was in an instant
the tying of a knot
in all the threads
of all the things: a knot
like a purple iris
tied in the highways,
the wars, desertifications,
the ripening wheat
around our homes
and the fireflies
in the blue-gold seeds,
the demolishing
collision of worlds,
the drawings away,
losses in the dark,
misery of childhood
in the poor house filled
with shouts and insects,
and then the new
moon of August—in all
threads of all things
a sudden knot, a
flower that speaks,
moves and dies
and came to meet me.

Every Body Broken

Every body broken. This
is hard to admit. Open the door. Admit
the bleeding stranger. Else
there never will be anyone with you in your house. This
is the only one there is.

This is your pounding, this is you
pounding, whining, cadging
to be admitted. Or lying,
lying there, a silence almost still,
with no word anymore except your body,
so that if no one will see
in your body what you're saying,
you'll never say anything again.

Every Step Was into a New World

Every step was into a new world
drenched in memory and longing: these were the dew there.
The sun sparkled in it, the low sun
that pierced the tips of the oak crowns
on the eastern, the far-side banks. A sparkling
that never would leave us, that later we'd know again
in the splendour of a breast shining in lace,
the stirring of birds by the creek,
the fluttering in our struck heart. The sun
shone through the drops of memory,
and the child was wet, chilled,
and warmed. The child we were.
He and she purred in nerves and muscles
and brought their eyes close to the places
they could see in the drops, some of the new worlds
of the spot where we'd halted for the morning.

The Last Thing

This dream is of doors open on streets
that twist away: canals
filled with the silver backs
of dolphins calling to be ridden,
ways drawn out of one another
through the intricate texture
of a jungle of glass and steel,
of fitted stones that change their colour
with the angles of sunlight, windows
looking on vegetable interiors,
stairways of vine, furniture
of trees grown into the forms
the human body casts outward, decoration
of flowers and fruit, painted sculpture,
and mixed scents carving a shape
in the mind. And the whole city
shifts steadily, as it has brought
me here to you, or you to me,
again, and so will tear apart
and reunite us after further adventure,
as this fable plays at playing out
all its proliferating hopes.

Here we can love even those tales
in which a vague foreboding
takes a body of coincidental death,
even those myths that explain motionlessness,
a man and woman lying side by side
helplessly, as a mirror
explains death. What difference
does such a thing make—like a dry oak that seems

to dominate a plain full of scattered groves—
to whatever is condensing in this twilight
to pour itself over us
from the pitcher of morning? We will wake
and drink and go away separately
or together through the streets, winding down
toward another season of sleep, aware
each day in the late afternoon
of a nearly invisible rumour, a shadow
bearing a letter from the rim of the hills.
Nothing is forgotten, and this shape
darkens as it approaches us, at last
taking on substance at its entrance
into our bodies. The distant sounds
are remembered suddenly for the voices
of the disembodied, which they were
in the days before this incarnating sleep.
And so we go on, always lightening, darkening,
in a secure and wild drama that once
in another life was reserved for the sky.

Author's Note and Acknowledgements

Michael Redhill made the selection for *The Sparrow* in a constant dialogue with me that I found stimulating and revealing. He worked by reading all my published poems and making his choices while consulting my own "much-too-long list," as we had to call it. Michael gentled me to the blood-boiling task of making a selection by his development of a clear, creative goal. Rather than being confused over what had to be omitted due to space (my method), we should concentrate on what *could* be present, rest happy with that, and apply a principle to choosing it. This was the idea that poems could be removed in such a way as to bring others into a closer, more intense relationship. Using the existing poems, we'd make a "selected" that was in fact a new book in my sequence, one that better exposed certain lines of force. I greatly liked this idea, and together Michael and I worked out its exact form, which is *The Sparrow*.

Acknowledgements of periodicals can be found in the original volumes, and so can notes detailing many of the poems' borrowings from sources. I long to acknowledge all the people who have helped me by welcoming my poetry over the years since 1966, when I first sent some of it into the world. Yet this would be just a list, and name-dropping. However, I not only long to but feel I must acknowledge the editors who have published the books that enable the present one to exist. Bruce Holsapple of Contraband Press. Robert MacDonald of Dreadnaught Inc. Allan Safarik of Blackfish Press, and Richard Teleky, then with Oxford University Press, who directed me to send Blackfish a manuscript of mine which, due to communication beyond my ken between Safarik and MacDonald, led to both *Black Orchid* and *Between the Root and the Flower*. Glynn Davies of Aya Press. John Hollander, who was outside poetry advisor for Princeton University Press when it accepted *The Tradition*. Maria Jacobs and Heather Cadsby of Wolsak and Wynn Publishers Ltd. Gilberto Meza, who translated a selection of my poems, put together *Ciudad interior*, and published it with the press of the Universidad Autónoma de Zacatecas.

Ron Hatch of Ronsdale Press (still Cacanadadada Press in the days of *Phantoms in the Ark*). The publishers and editors of limited editions and chapbooks which were absorbed in whole or part into later volumes: Robyn Sarah, Fred Louder, Jack Hannan, Alexandre Amprimoz, Joan Latchford, Caryl Peters, Shane Nielson, Dan Wells, Salvatore Ala, Agnes Cserhati. Richard Olafson of Ekstasis Editions. My editors at Brick Books, Don McKay, Jan Zwicky, and John Donlan, and Brick's managing editor, Kitty Lewis. All of the many who founded, and were, the anarchist poets publishing collective watershedBooks, which we operated for five years, publishing eleven volumes, including my *The End of the Age*: especially those members who were and are my close friends and who worked on that book, Allan Briesmaster, Pierre L'Abbé, and Steve McCabe. Paul Vermeersch, now Senior Editor at Wolsak and Wynn, who proposed the idea of *Early Poems* and published it when he was operating his imprint 4 A.M. Books at Insomniac Press. Sarah MacLachlan, Matt Williams, and all who have made Anansi a belovèd literary home for me since 2002, when we began working towards *Night Street Repairs*. As with watershedBooks, so with Anansi, it's impossible for me to name all of the many people who in various capacities have supported and enabled my books and have been friends to me. But in addition to Sarah and Matt, I want to mention former Anansi chief editors Martha Sharpe, Lynn Henry, and Jared Bland; former managing editor Kelly Joseph and managing editor Maria Golikova; former poetry editor Damian Rogers; and present poetry editor Kevin Connolly. I owe special gratitude to the substantive editors who did so much to shape the books, chiefly my friend Ken Babstock, who was an indispensable partner in giving final form to *Night Street Repairs*, *The Sentinel*, and *The New Measures*. For *The New Measures*, Jared Bland also played a vital editorial role, as did Damian Rogers on *Sequence*, and it was she who took Sarah's earlier desire for a selected poems and brought it to me again and got me to accept it as the real next thing. Editors are said to "acquire" books. I want to return to my earliest Anansi friends, and say that it was Ken who contrived, and Sarah and Martha who oversaw, the acquisition of *me*. I'm eternally grateful.

Author photograph by Steve Payne

A. F. MORITZ has written nineteen books of poetry. His work has received the Griffin Poetry Prize, the Guggenheim Fellowship, the Award in Literature of the American Academy of Arts and Letters, *Poetry* magazine's Bess Hokin Prize, the Ingram Merrill Fellowship, the ReLit Award, and the Raymond Souster Award, and he has three times been a finalist for the Governor General's Literary Award. His Griffin Poetry Prize–winning collection, *The Sentinel*, was a *Globe and Mail* Top 100 Book of the Year, and his ReLit Award–winning *Night Street Repairs* was named one of forty-three "books of the decade" by the *Globe and Mail* in 2010. He lives in Toronto.